RED LIGHTS & BEYOND
"DEATH, DYING & DESTRUCTION"

A Collection of True Short Stories of Fire-EMS,
Air Medical, and the Medical Examiner's Office

David B. Pope, Retired
FIRE-EMS CAPTAIN
FLIGHT PARAMEDIC
MEDICOLEGAL DEATH INVESTIGATOR

DEDICATION

This book is dedicated to the memory of the many departed souls who passed through my hands over a period of 35 years, and to all the dispatchers and first responders, including fire-EMS and law enforcement, for their fearless work in the field.

Also, to my family, for enduring the many missed birthdays, ball games, anniversaries, holidays, and meals. Those missed events allowed me to perform a valuable service to our community, our state, and at times even our nation. I thank them dearly for their understanding and their constant support.

PREFACE

My name is David B. Pope. I retired from a fire-emergency medical services (EMS) department consisting of eight medic units, twelve engine companies, and four ladder companies. During any given 24-hour shift, there would also be two battalion chiefs and one EMS captain on duty. My role was that of EMS captain. I supervised the emergency medical portion of the shift and took part in the fire-side operations.

I started out as a volunteer firefighter in a rural department in the late 1970s. I was soon drawn to the world of emergency medical services and achieved a Nationally Registered Emergency Medical Technician-Ambulance (NREMT-A) certification, which was the basic level of training, in 1981. I then went on to become a Shock Trauma Technician (EMT-ST) in 1982, a Cardiac Technician (EMT-CT) in 1983, and a NREMT-Paramedic in 1984. I became gainfully employed as a paramedic on the streets of a city with a population of approximately 100,000 in 1985.

During my time as a paramedic, I taught numerous classes at both a local health science college and the department where I worked. These classes included Cardiopulmonary Resuscitation (CPR), Pre-Hospital Trauma Life Support (PHTLS), Pediatric Advanced Life Support (PALS), and Advanced Cardiac Life Support (ACLS), among others. I also held certifications in a multitude of fire, EMS, Federal Emergency Management Agency (FEMA), and death investigator courses. I was also a flight paramedic for approximately seven years with the local Level I Trauma Center.

After retiring from the city in 2010, I applied for, and was hired as, a medicolegal death investigator with the State Office of the Chief Medical Examiner (OCME). During the application process, I was asked how many death scenes I had attended. It took a while, but I did the math and came up with about 4,500. I think that, and my medical background, got me the job. After two years with the OCME, I was required to pass the American Board of Medicolegal Death Investigators (ABMDI) certification, which I did and stayed with the ME's office for a little over four years. Then I hung it up. If you have not already noticed, my life has involved a bunch of acronyms for approximately 30 years, trying to save people. But the last four, not so much— I was done. I find it cathartic to write these words and relive the emotion of those times.

The following stories are all painfully true. However, sort of like they used say on Dragnet, the names and places were changed to protect the, well, innocent doesn't apply in every situation. The names and places were changed due to health information privacy laws and to protect the insane, the absurd, and the not-so-innocent, as well as the innocent.

I hope you enjoy. — D.B.P

TABLE OF CONTENTS

INCIDENT ONE:
"THE FLOOD OF THE CENTURY"

I had been gainfully employed as a paramedic for just under a year and had just arrived for my eight-hour shift. During the time it took to get a shift change report from Jeff, the medic I was replacing, the dispatcher came over the radio and advised us of a cardiac call less than three miles from our station. Jeff jumped into the driver's seat, and I rode shotgun. We raced to the scene with lights flashing and siren blaring.

It had been raining for several days, hard at times, but nothing to write home about. Apparently, the remnants of a hurricane had stalled on top of our city for a day or so, dumping five or six inches of rain. Another storm was right behind that one and it decided to park for a while, as well. No one in the city was even remotely prepared for what happened over the next several days.

Our fledgling City Emergency Service Operations was just getting started. We were an Advanced Life Support agency and our equipment was sufficient to handle most medical emergencies, but that was pretty much it. The career side worked hand-in-hand with volunteer crew members. There would normally be one career paramedic and one volunteer Emergency Medical Technician (EMT) driver, in an ambulance. Additional assistance was few and far between. Sarah, the crew's First lieutenant, was to be my volunteer EMT driver for the day. She arrived shortly after Jeff, and I took off for the call. She followed soon after in a response vehicle.

As we drove farther up the street we noticed an unusual amount of water but continued driving. The water levels eventually forced us over to the left lane. We then had to cross the median and proceed up the opposing one-way lanes. The situation still didn't click for us. We had the cardiac case on our minds and, until a bit later, had no idea how screwed we really were.

There was a large parking lot in front of a shopping center on the south side of Primrose Avenue, and we drove up into it to escape the rising water— however our cardiac call was on the other side of the road. Jeff and I waded across the street and started making our way to our patient. I remember Jeff had a Lifepak-5 cardiac monitor/defibrillator, along with an oxygen tank. I was packing the drug box and a large jump kit. I also had our only radio in a holster attached to my belt. Bear in mind, this was long before smart phones, or even flip-phones were in use.

Jeff and I were walking on the far side when he fell, submerging the Lifepak, which meant we wouldn't be able to evaluate the patient's heart via electrocardiogram or EKG. He got up. Moments later, I went down. There was no doubt now—the radio was toast. Our day was not going as planned. By this time, Sarah had arrived. She was back in the parking lot and stayed with the medic unit.

The business where our patient waited for us was conveniently up a small hill and high and dry, at least for the moment. We arrived and began assessing the man. He appeared to be having a simple panic attack. We continued to notice the water rising outside at an alarming rate. We finished checking out the patient and, determining he was not in danger, advised him and the others in the business to stay put and not try to get out through the rising water.

Jeff and I made it back across the flooded street where we caught up with Sarah. People were trying to drive through the floodwaters and across a small bridge, but their cars were stalling. We notified dispatch that we had no idea what was happening in other parts of the city, but we needed additional manpower, as well as boats, life jackets, ropes, and anything else they could muster. Between 25-35 people were trapped in and around the intersection of Moore's Creek and Primrose Avenue.

Unfortunately, almost the entire city seemed to be on the verge of going under water. We started pulling people out of the cars closest to us, and enlisted civilians to form human chains to reach cars that were farther away.

I heard a young man yelling that he couldn't swim and needed help. It looked like he was standing in four or five feet of water and holding onto the side of a building. I believed I could wade over to him and walk him back to safety before the water got too high. I told Sarah I was going over to get him, and I started to carefully work my way across the road as it was rapidly turning into a river, while trying not to fall into a manhole. There were many things floating in the water—some potentially hazardous.

Halfway across, I realized the water was too deep for wading and I needed to swim. I had on a cotton jumpsuit with heavy work boots, which were a liability in that situation. I held my breath and went under the muddy flood water to remove the boots and let them go. At least then I could swim a bit easier. I was too close to the young man to turn around, so I continued across what was now a wide river. The only thing that made it manageable was the current was not too strong. The little creek that had become a raging torrent was running away from us, and we were in the backwash.

By this time, the young man was frantic. I was about 25 feet from him when something blindsided me. I turned to see a floating car had hit me in the back. I finally got to the young man and found that he wasn't standing in just a few feet of water but was actually on top of a three-foot wall. The floodwaters were about eight feet deep and carrying cars, fifty-gallon barrels of God knows what and anything else that could float.

I told him to try to stay calm. That didn't work all that well. The guy was terrified, and, honestly, I did not feel great, either. This was in early November, and brother let me tell you—that damn water was cold and nasty!

4

I could barely hear Sarah yelling and could not make out what she was saying. I found out later she saw me go under and didn't see me come back up until I made it to the wall where the seventeen-year-old was standing. She told me she thought I was gone.

Meanwhile, she and Jeff were still working with the civilians to rescue people who had grabbed hold of cars, signs, telephone poles, and anything else they could find.

I didn't know if anyone was going to be able to get to us, so I tried to come up with a self-rescue plan. The young man was terrified and couldn't swim, so trying to keep him calm was critical. The only thing we had to hold onto was a small electrical sconce on the side of the building. Thank God the power was out. Every once in a while, he would try to hold onto me, or climb and pull me under. I shook him hard and yelled, "I swam over here; I can swim back! Don't do that again!" What he didn't know was that, by that point, I was so cold I couldn't have made it back.

A 50-gallon barrel of something floated within reach, and I grabbed it. I told my new friend to hold onto the bottom edge of the barrel and I would do the same on the opposite side, then try to kick my legs to float us out. We moved about 15 or 20 feet from our perch before he panicked and tried to climb on the barrel. I grabbed him and swam back to the temporary safety of the wall.

It was really not looking great for either of us, and we were both shivering uncontrollably. I'm not sure how long he had been in the water, but it had been at least 45 minutes since I had left the opposite shore.

I looked up a few minutes later to see Hank—another one of our medics—in a rowboat heading toward us. He looked like an angel. Hank pulled up to us and helped the young man into the boat, and then me. I'm not sure he realized how desperate we were, but he saved our lives. He rowed back to where Jeff and Sarah were, and, if memory serves, there were some strong hugs.

Oddly enough, the uniform shop where the city had bought our jump suits was in that shopping center. I walked in and told them I needed some warm dry clothes and to charge it to the city's account. God bless them—they quickly obliged. They even had socks and boots! They also made a fresh pot of hot coffee which hit the spot. I left that place one happy camper.

Unfortunately, that feeling didn't last long.

The young man I had befriended in the water was placed in a warm medic unit and transported to the hospital. He had hypothermia, but he recuperated from his near-death experience.

There were still many people in that newly made river we had to help. The boat made it easier to get to some of them, but there were others who did not fare as well. I remember watching a yellow Ford Pinto turn upside down in the torrent and go over the side of the small bridge. The young lady inside was screaming and clawing at the window as she disappeared with the car. I ran down the side of the muddy monster and could see the car strike a tree and then float out of sight.

We found the car with the girl still inside two days later.

We also found an elderly lady nearby wrapped backwards around a tree. I suppose she had also gone over the bridge, unnoticed at the time. A baby was found about four days after the flood. It turned out that she had been in that yellow Ford Pinto, as well. We didn't know the girl in the car had a baby. But even if we had known, nothing would have changed.

Seven more inches of rain fell that day. Rescues were taking place throughout the area. Helicopters pulled people off submerged buildings that collapsed as the last people were rescued. We commandeered several boats from a dealership and put them into service with anyone who could drive one.

We pulled people off the tops of buildings, out of second-story windows, and from floating cars. If there was a place someone could get out of the water, we found them there.

One of our fellow medics—Joe—had gone under when his boat capsized and was not seen coming back up. Three others in that boat safely made it to dry land. We had been told he was considered missing somewhere in the muddy waters. We knew the chances of him surviving were at best a long shot. But damn if he didn't. He had held onto a tree downstream until the water subsided enough for him to walk out.

That lucky son of a bitch!

During three days of flooding, 12 people were lost in our area. In my opinion, the citizens were lucky the number was that low. Now, this is only from my perspective, but during those horrifying days, all the men and women working with fire, EMS, police, dispatch, National Guard, and Air Medical, as well as all the personnel in the hospitals and the citizens who volunteered just because they were needed, worked long and hard hours to save an untold number of lives throughout the region. It was a widespread event that taught all of us valuable lessons about how to prepare for and handle inevitable future disasters.

A personal note: There are things that one cannot unsee, and if I had ever taken my job lightly, after that flood I would never do so again.

INCIDENT TWO:
"BORN IN THE CAUL"

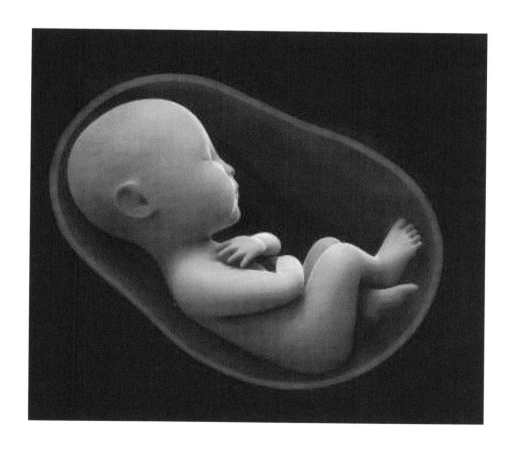

"A lass if born in June with a caul
Will wed, hev bairns and rear 'em all.
But a lass if born with a caul in July,
Will lose her caul and young will die.
Every month beside luck comes with a caul
If safe put by,
If lost she may cry:
For ill luck on her will fall.
For man it's luck—be born when he may—
It is safe be kept ye mind,
But if lost it be he'll find
Ill-deed his lot for many a day."
(John Fairfax-Blakeborough, 1923)

"Suddenly, with an electronic click, the florescent lights in the ceiling flooded the room with a bright, annoying glow as the emergency tones blared, once again signaling that a call was about to be announced."

Our alert system had three types of tones. One was for announcements, and two others were for emergencies—fire calls and EMS calls. This one was an EMS call. As the EMS supervisor, I realized my chances for more sleep that night was over.

The dispatcher spoke succinctly over the loudspeakers: "Engine-8, Medic-7, and RS-1 (Rescue Supervisor-1) respond to 2302 Colonial Avenue Southwest for a woman in labor. Contractions are only two minutes apart. Go to channel three, 05:24."

It had already been a long night. The tones had sounded five or six times, and the sleep lost would never be found. I had just fallen asleep as the clock ticked softly in the background. The change from A-shift to B-shift was only 90 minutes away. The end of a 24-hour shift was always a needed and welcomed moment to a weary Fire-EMS captain.

I threw my legs over the side of the bed, slid my feet into my boots, and pulled up the bunker pants that had been draped over the boots. As I was pulling the suspenders over my shoulders, I made my way to the polished brass fire pole leading to the apparatus bay. Wrapping my legs around it, I slid down through the hole in the floor, landing softly on the rubber pad at the bottom. As I wiped away the small amount of sleep that had accumulated on my eyes, the dispatcher repeated, "Engine-8, Medic-7, RS-1, respond to 2302 Colonial Avenue Southwest for a woman in labor." But this time added, "We have been informed the baby is crowning and that this is the woman's fifth delivery. Go to channel three, 05:25."

This let us know that either the baby would be born prior to our arrival, or we would be playing midwife in a few short minutes. When I heard dispatch mention it was the patient's fifth delivery, I said out loud, "Crowning, hell. She'll probably just squirt this one out."

Little did I know how close I was to the truth.

I went over to the printer in the apparatus bay. It's where we received information such as the address and nature of a call and any adjunct comments. There was an acknowledgement button—known as the mushroom button because of its shape—we were supposed to push to let the dispatcher know we had received the call.

Printout in hand, I headed over to RS-1's apparatus bay. RS-1 was a 2007 diesel-powered Chevy 2500 pickup truck. It was loaded to the gills with fire and EMS equipment—pretty much anything you needed to respond to a call—plus several specialized pieces of equipment for advanced life support or mass-casualty incidents.

As I walked past the garage door, I pressed the opener so the bay would be open when I climbed into the vehicle. I started the engine of the Chevy and pulled out of the garage. I informed the dispatcher I was en route and transferring my radio traffic to the assigned channel. I clicked on the red and white strobe lights and hit the siren as I left the parking lot.

It had been 70 seconds since the fluorescent lights woke me up.

Meanwhile, I prepared myself mentally for the task ahead, while flashing back to calls that had not gone well. Losing a child is unspeakably traumatic for parents. But it is also difficult for fire and EMS personnel.

The dimly lit streets were beginning to come to life as I continued to respond. Though early morning commuters can sometimes be harried, on this day, for some reason, they were pulling out of my way.

Approximately halfway to the address, dispatch advised the baby had just been delivered—but that the mother's water had not broken yet. I acknowledged and began to process the information, while dodging other vehicles. Many scenarios and questions darted through my mind. How could the mother have delivered without her water breaking? Should I call the dispatchers and have them tell the woman to expose the baby from the amniotic sac? Or should I deal with it when I arrived?

I was only a minute or so out, so I decided to wait and not assume anything. I continued racing down the road. Three minutes and thirty-four seconds into the response, all three units arrived simultaneously. Over the radio, I heard Engine-8 on scene and Medic-7 arriving on scene. I advised dispatch that RS-1 was on scene. Dispatch acknowledged the radio traffic. It was now 05:28.

Less than five minutes had passed since the tones sounded at the station.

Seeing personnel from the fire engine and medic unit gathering the necessary equipment, I proceeded to the front of the house. As I entered, I was confronted with something I had never seen during all my years on the streets.

It was not uncommon to arrive to find a baby already born and nestled in its mother's arms. In those cases, the medic would suction the child's mouth and nose, clamp the umbilical cord in two places a few inches apart, wait for the cord to stop pulsating, cut it between the two clamps, then encourage the mother to nurse the baby, which facilitates delivery of the placenta and helps prevent internal bleeding.

Some of this was going on—but there was a twist.

The baby—a girl—had been born and was in the mother's arms, but the baby was still completely enclosed in the amniotic fluid sac, and the umbilical cord was still attached to the placenta. Another strange thing about the situation was that the placenta was torn, partially delivered, and lying on the mother's abdomen.

The baby looked like a squirrel inside a clear balloon.

The 27-year -old was yelling, "My baby's not breathing!" She was right. I told her I was there to help. The baby had to be removed from the fluid before she could breathe. I said something to the effect that the baby was still swimming, and we had to remove it from the pool before it would start to breathe. The official term for this is being "born in the caul". This occurs in only one out of 80,000 cases.

The dangerous part was that the placenta had also been delivered, and we did not know how long it had been since the child's lifeline had been cut. One of the other medics broke out the obstetrics kit which included a bulb syringe, scalpel, and a couple of umbilical clamps. I tore the amniotic fluid sac, exposing her small, wrinkled, pale blue face and body to her first contact with the world as we know it. The mother flinched as warm fluid drained across her abdomen. I depressed the end of the bulb syringe and placed it in the infant's throat to remove the fluid that had kept the embryo and then the fetus warm and secure for so long. That fluid now posed a danger, for what the baby now needed more than anything else in the world—was air.

I suctioned her nostrils and dried the baby with a towel, wrapping her so she could be warm that cold February morning. I rubbed her little feet and legs and then her head again. I suctioned one more time. I heard a small whimper as she opened her tiny eyes to see the new world. Sadly, I was the first thing she saw.

Thankfully, she won't remember that.

Realizing her baby seemed to be alright, the mother looked closer and exclaimed, "It's a girl!"

I continued my assessment of the premature baby. Her respiration rate had not increased as it should. I continued to stimulate the child to try to get her to breathe faster. I placed a stethoscope on her tiny chest and listened for her heartbeat. I calculated it at the rate of 160 per minute.

That was a good sign.

I then used a bag valve mask to assist her breathing. This helped her skin change from pale blue to a healthier pink color. This meant her lungs were starting to exchange bad air for good. But all was not well just yet. She needed to move more air and faster. I decided to take her to the emergency department without the mother. I continued to assist her breathing on the way to the hospital. Another medic unit was called in to assist and transport the mother.

I asked one of the fire fighters to crank up the heat in the back of the ambulance to make it as warm as possible for the baby. I cradled the little girl in my arms and made my way to the unit. I looked at the driver and said, "OK, let's go!"

En route to the hospital, I continued to assist the baby's breathing until her respiratory rate increased to an acceptable level and her skin color improved. I then cut the O2 line, allowing the flow of oxygen to flush the baby's face. This is called "flow by O2," and it enriches the oxygen content in the baby's lungs.

I continued to stimulate the baby to get her to react the way I knew she should. I got her to grimace at one point, which was a good reaction. I called the hospital and told them we were en route with a newborn premature baby, and she was experiencing some respiratory distress. I gave an Apgar score—a ten-point scale for assessing the health of newborns—of four a minute after birth and six at ten minutes. Neither score is considered good, but the baby was slowly improving.

When we got to the ED, I walked in holding the baby close to my chest. She was wrapped in warm towels, and oxygen was flowing across her tiny face. I handed her to the nurse who then placed the baby on the scales. She said, "Oh my God, she is so tiny—two pounds four ounces."

For the first time in several minutes, I was able to step back, relax, and reflect on what had happened. I had participated in the birth of many babies during my career. Most had done very well, but some had not.

This one was special.

I called the hospital the next day and spoke to the physician caring for the baby. He appreciated my call. He told me she was doing very well, and her prognosis was good. I told him that, over the years, I had seen so many people check out that it was refreshing to see one checking in.

INCIDENT THREE:
"FLIGHT INTO THE UNKNOWN"

It was another run of the mill day for the hospital's air ambulance crew: — a pilot, flight nurse, and flight medic. They sat around the office, reading a bit from yet another flight safety manual, maybe played a joke or two on the pilot, and caught the news on the television. Then a call came in for a site response at a school in the next county.

As a flight medic—and a father— I always had in the back of my mind the thought, *"What if the next flight is for one of my kids?"* That would be devastating. That frightening thought came to mind that day because the request came from the same EMS agency that I used to run with and covered the school that my kids attended. They requested that our helicopter land on the school's baseball field.

A victim had apparently been hit by a car.

Let me set the stage. The school house was near the ballfield, and the road was next to that—all in plain view of one another. They had set up a landing zone with fire trucks standing by. My mind continued to churn with "what if" thoughts. As I made ready for the flight, I had to call on my training to overcome my fear of the unknown. The pilot made a quick check of weather conditions and gave a thumbs-up as we all made our way to the helipad. The twin-engine Bell 412 was all decked out in red, white, and blue. All four blades drooped down like branches of a huge oak tree.

The nurse climbed through the side door opening, and the pilot slid onto his perch on the right side of the craft. My role at this point was to connect the auxiliary power unit (APU) to the nose of the aircraft and wait until the batteries sufficiently cranked the engines and the rotors began to whip through the air with a "thump, thump, thump, thump" sound that grew louder and louder. I was thankful for hearing protection.

After the bird was up to speed, I detached the APU and rolled it to the side of the helipad. I then took my place in the left "co-pilot" seat, secured my four-point restraints, plugged my communications cable into the radio system, and gave the pilot a thumbs up. We were good to go.

Over the intercom, the pilot advised the crew of imminent takeoff. He then radioed the local air traffic control tower: "Life Flight 412 Charlie Mike departing the hospital en route to Castlebrook for a site response." The Lifeguard designation advises the tower and flight is an emergency and requires priority. The tower told him to proceed and gave him a safe altitude. As the giant bird shot up into the air, buildings that once towered over us became smaller and insignificant.

When we were about 15 minutes away, we contacted the fire department at the landing zone (LZ). They advised that the patient was not a victim of a hit-and-run but of a gunshot wound—self-inflicted. At first, that made no sense, but after I learned more about the circumstances, I understood the confusion. I also felt a sigh of relief, and then a twinge of guilt because of my relief. I knew my kids were young and did not have access to a gun. As we approached the LZ, we saw three emergency vehicles forming a triangle toward the center of the ballfield with their lights flashing. At first, they looked like toy trucks from a "Hot Wheels" box. As they grew in size during our approach, so did our sense of urgency.

We landed softly on the green grass outlining the bases. Dust whipped, biting the unprotected faces of people on the field. I looked toward the school. Though my kids were safe, they were no doubt among the students with noses pressed to windows and innocent eyes watching the drama unfold on the field where they ran and played.

Our attention then turned toward the subject who was already in the back of the ambulance. The volunteer crew had their patient face down on the stretcher due to his compromised airway. I climbed into the ambulance and took my position at the patient's head. I placed my hands on either side of his head with my arms crossed. In this position, when we turned him on his back, I would have his face directly in front of me. This position would be optimal for maintaining care of his airway and breathing, as well as to continue cervical spine stabilization.

The patient, who to my surprise was apparently still conscious, was becoming more and more agitated due to hypoxia. The blood was pouring over his vocal cords and causing them to spasm and close, cutting off his air supply. On the count of three, the nurse, myself, and a couple of the volunteer crew members turned the patient faceup. To my initial shock, his face was gone…missing…basically, shot off! Soon thereafter, I leaned that the weapon of choice had been a .30-30 rifle placed under the chin. I could see his vocal cords without equipment. We secured his neck as best we could with half of a cervical collar, and I began to suction the blood from the ragged open wound that encompassed the major portion of his face. Soon after we had turned him to a supine position his agitation grew and grew. I knew in order to appropriately treat him during the flight I would have to have absolute control over his airway, but every time I tried to insert an endotracheal tube, his vocal cords slammed shut like a trap door.

A few years later, a technique that allows you to sedate and then intubate the patient would be used. Unfortunately, that was not an option with our current protocols.

I noticed that he appeared to be looking at me with the one unaffected eye, and I heard someone mention his name, and my disbelief was almost overwhelming…I knew him! I had known him for years. He and his parents went to the same church that my family attended. I called his name. He opened the only eye I could find, and I asked him if he knew who I was. He tried to nod as if to say yes. I told him I was going to have to insert an artificial airway into his neck so that I could help him breathe during our flight to the trauma center. He simply tried to nod again, but at the same time, I believe fear had already overtaken his thoughts.

I took a three-inch twelve-gauge angiocath and inserted it through his cricothyroid membrane—just below what is commonly known as the Adams apple—and advanced the catheter into his trachea. I honestly don't believe he felt the needle at all. I then attached an appliance known as a transtracheal jet insufflator (TTJI) that was in turn attached to an oxygen tank and began to assist his respirations. He calmed almost instantaneously. My partner, a highly trained flight nurse, was starting two large-bore intravenous (IV) catheters and had already attached the EKG monitor as well as a pulse oximetry probe. We transferred our patient to the helicopter and began the relatively short flight back to the hospital.

I remember wondering how much of this my sons had seen from their classroom. I could hardly believe our patient had been conscious all this time and stayed conscious throughout the flight. I spoke to him, in an attempt to reassure him that we were going to take good care of him, and I tried to prepare him for what he was about to encounter in the trauma room. I explained that he would see a large group of people and very bright lights and that he would be poked and stuck and that it was all for his own good.

It's sometimes very difficult to tell the same story over and over again in an attempt to reassure a patient when you know they are about to go through another stage of hell.

Miraculously, his blood pressure and heart rate as well as his oxygen saturation remained stable during the flight. I didn't really believe his brain could withstand the trauma from a point-blank discharge from a .30-30 rifle. I later found out that the bullet had exited the forehead and did not directly contact any portion of the brain but had caused extensive bone and tissue damage to the jaw and face.

We landed gently on the helipad, and the crew from the awaiting ambulance was ready with their stretcher. Due to the severity of his injury, this was to be a "hot unload." This simply meant we would not wait for the rotors to stop churning. The wind from the downdraft was driving toward the ground at approximately sixty miles per hour as we moved from the bird to the ambulance. I maintained a secure hold on the patient's head to try to control his cervical spine and, at the same time, maintain his airway. We were now only a two-minute drive from the trauma center. We unloaded the blood-soaked stretcher and rolled into the trauma room where awaited an array of caretakers, including trauma surgeons, an anesthesiologist, and a multitude of other physicians as well as a number of highly trained nurses, respiratory techs, and scribes.

As we entered the room, I started my verbal turnover to the staff. "We have a 17-year-old male with a self-inflicted GSW (gunshot wound) to the jaw and face. The weapon was a .30-30 rifle. We bandaged as best we could after I did a TTJI on scene due to extreme hypoxia and inability to intubate." The nurses removed the blood-soaked bandages on his face to reveal what can only be described as "hamburger." His jaw was missing, his nose was gone, only one eye was visible, and God help him, he was still conscious and looking around. I advised the trauma team of everything we had done, and the flight nurse updated them on his vital signs. At that point, a respiratory tech took over assisting his ventilations. I walked out of the trauma room, leaned against the wall, and began to openly sob. I had worked on a lot of people over the years and several GSWs to the face, but this one was different. I knew him, I knew his parents, and my emotions simply poured out.

He survived and, as much as possible, I followed his progress. I'm not sure how many reconstructive surgeries he endured but many would be a gross understatement. He went on to finish college and became a teacher.

I lost touch with him over the years, but one Christmas, many years later, a card came in the mail. I opened it, and to my complete shock, as I read the card, my emotions flowed throughout my body as if that flight from the school ballfield had just ended. The card read, "Mr. Pope, Merry Christmas! I hope you and your family are doing well. I'm fine, just looking forward to the possibility of snow for Christmas! I don't know if I ever said this but, thank you for everything that you did for me." He then made another comment about the flight that was important to me, but personal enough for me not to share. He then said once again, thank you and Merry Christmas! I still have and dearly cherish that Christmas card. The emotions I feel as I type these words are difficult to explain.

INCIDENT FOUR:

"THE LEG"

One night fairly early in my EMS career, I had finally fallen asleep when the alarm went out for a motorcycle accident with the rider's leg cut off! The call location was only about three blocks from the station.

One will not appreciate the gravity of the situation without a bit of background. Rodney, my volunteer EMT driver had a bad history of abusing Valium, as well as other habits I prefer to not mention. I went to his bunk to wake him, and I could not. I went so far as to drag him from his bed onto the floor and still Rodney continued to snore. He was sleeping like a freaking baby.

As luck would have it, my friend Frank, another paramedic, was spending the night at the crew hall to avoid his wife (an entirely different story). I told him I needed him to drive. He thankfully accepted the offer, and we drove with lights and siren to the scene.

Keep in mind that when dispatch relays information from a bystander, the info is quite often inaccurate. When told by dispatch that the man's leg had been cut off, we thought it was more like a bad laceration.

As we pulled up to the patient, he was thrashing about on the ground with his stub in the air. His left leg from mid-thigh down was missing, and he was bleeding profusely. He had reportedly struck a telephone pole during his crash. On scene, a police officer was standing by and maintaining control over the immediate area.

Frank and I went to the patient, and as he was assessing the patient's ABCs (airway, breathing and circulation), I attended to the obvious circulation problem. Sometimes even bad wounds clot off easily; however, this one did not. I placed a trauma pack on the stump and attached a tourniquet just above the amputation. This was also the days when MAST (Military Anti-Shock Trousers) were popular, and I applied MAST to stabilize his lower extremities and pelvis. I asked the police officer if he knew where the leg was and he stated, "It's over by the telephone pole." I then asked the officer to wrap it up in a clean sheet and place it in the medic unit. His eyes got as big as saucers, and he walked away.

A non-rebreather mask was applied with high flow oxygen as well as an EKG. I popped in a fourteen-gauge IV with Ringer's lactate solution into his arm, and we took off for the hospital. The young man remained conscious throughout transport to the emergency department (ED), and he did rather well.

While en route, I advised the hospital what we had, as well as what we had done for the patient. A trauma alert was called by the ED, and that alerted all the staff necessary to properly take care of this type of patient.

Upon arrival to the ED, Frank and I wheeled the patient into the trauma room, and I gave a verbal turnover to the waiting group of doctors, nurses, and respiratory staff.

When they took over, I advised that I had brought the severed limb and went to the medic unit to retrieve it. I looked in between the front seats and in the floor of the back of the unit, but the leg was nowhere to be found. I then noticed a bloody sheet on the bench where I had been sitting. You guessed it; it was belted in on the seat. I placed the leg under my arm with the foot sticking out of the end of the sheet and started back to the ED.

The ED entrance was in a dimly lit breezeway, and as I approached the entrance a man dressed in scrubs was coming from the opposite direction. I waved the foot at the guy and said, "Can you give me a hand? I already have a foot." With that said, the guy called me a nut, and I concurred, and took the leg to the room where our patient was being treated. I found out later that unfortunately they were not able to reattach "The Leg."

27

INCIDENT FIVE:
"MAYDAY! MAYDAY!"

Just another wonderful day in the life. Nothing remarkable was going on until a fire call went out. "Tone, Tone, Tone. Engine-1, Ladder-1, Medic-1, Engine-7, Medic-7, Battalion -1, and RS-1 respond to a structure fire 2701 Marshall Avenue." As Rescue Supervisor, I covered the entire city. We had two battalion chiefs (BCs) who split the city's responsibility. When this call rang out, I happened to be pretty far away, so I marked that I was en route, flicked on my red lights and siren, and hit the gas.

I listened on the radio as the first engine company arriving on the scene reported a two-story wood frame structure with smoke and flames showing. Knowing L-1, M-1, and BC-1 were right behind them, E-1 decided to make entry and take their own water. Again, being aware that they had others about to arrive that can lay water lines and get them additional water very soon. BC-1 arrived, assumed command of the scene, and began to give assignments on the radio. I listened to the assignments being called out, and E-7 assisted with the interior fire attack.

I was about one minute out from the scene, when I heard at first, faintly, "Mayday, Mayday." Then louder, and with a major sense of urgency...MAYDAY!!! MAYDAY!!! FIREFIGHTER DOWN!!! At that point, everyone on the scene was working toward one goal — saving the life of the downed firefighter.

I had no idea who was in trouble, but I knew all of them and had worked with most of them for years. I have to admit, I probably broke several of the department's standard operating procedures on the rest of my response.

I arrived on the scene to see several of my co-worker's performing CPR and trying to manage the firefighter's airway. Keep in mind, this firefighter was extremely well known and liked. He had been with the department for several years, and he was in deep trouble.

The firefighter working his close friends airway was having some difficulty with his emotions, so I kind of eased in and took over the patient's airway. That would have been my duty regardless of who the patient was at the time.

The downed firefighter's captain had been with him when he simply collapsed while fighting the fire. The captain brought him out to the porch and a couple of others took him into the yard and started working on him. With no pulse and not breathing, he was in full cardiac arrest.

I have to say, he could not have picked a better place to code. He had EMTs and paramedics all over him. I was ventilating him as others were performing cardiac compressions, monitoring his EKG, starting an IV, and administering medications.

Suddenly, he went into ventricular fibrillation (V-fib). The squeal of the defibrillator (d-fib) paddles charging became apparent, and then…CLEAR, CLEAR rang out and a shock was delivered as his limp body jerked violently. His heart started back, and he became slightly combative, which is very common in that kind of situation. We got him loaded into the medic unit and started transporting to the ED. Shortly after we marked en route, our firefighter, our co-worker, our friend, coded again. His heart went back into V-fib and once again he was shocked. When he became unconscious again, I tried to intubate, but he came around after the d-fib and I stayed with using the bag valve mask. We arrived at the hospital and our patient was alive, but everything was extremely iffy at that point. I was standing beside him in the emergency room, and he looked at me and said something to the effect of, "What the fuck are you doing here?" and I realized he was back with us. I don't think I have ever felt so elated.

The little son of a gun not only recovered from his cardiac event, but he went back with the fire department and worked until retirement and is still doing extremely well to this day. One for the good guys.

INCIDENT SIX:
"TWO OUT OF THREE AIN'T BAD"

Why stupid people do stupid things at zero-dark-hundred hours, I'll never figure out. We were sleeping like babies when…you guessed it…the tones RANG OUT. The dispatcher followed: "Engine-4, Medic-4, RS-1 respond to 5301 Benton Road Northeast for a Code 44, shooting." The location was no more than four blocks from Station 4. So, Engine-4 and Medic-4 advised dispatch they were en route, on scene, and standing by for the police department (PD) all at the same time. They had not even yet pulled out of the apparatus bay. I had about a five-minute response and arrived at Station 4 prior to PD securing the scene.

When people are shooting at each other, EMS personnel really don't like to get in the middle of it. After all, the only thing we have for protection is a pair of scissors or maybe a flashlight. Sometimes we do accidentally get in the way but, fortunately, not this time.

Shortly after PD had marked on scene, they advised it was safe and to come on in. By that time we were about a block out, so we approached and marked on scene. As EMS Supervisor, I arrived in one vehicle and Medic-4 and Engine-4 were right behind me.

Anytime one approaches the scene of a shooting, one must maintain a high degree of vigilance. It is comforting to a point that the police are there and have the scene as secure as they can, but that does not mean one can let down one's guard. Therefore, the approach needs to be steady but not rushed, with eyes wide open and situational awareness a must.

I approached the house, and there were already two or three police cars in the street. I saw an officer at the top of a set of outside steps signaling for me to come in. I walked up the steps to find a twentyish female holding her neck with a considerable amount of blood on her neck and shirt. The officer advised me that there were two more inside. That basically put me in triage mode, and the medic unit and engine personnel, consisting of two paramedics and four EMTs, would take care of immediate treatment. I quickly assessed the young lady on the steps and deemed her to be a "Green" patient.

In medical triage, you have four basic types of patients: "Green" being the walking wounded, not serious; "Yellow" being potentially serious but not immediate; "Red" being life-threatening condition and in need of immediate treatment; and "Black" being deceased, no treatment required.

I continued into the house where the officer was directing me as one of the other paramedics and an EMT from Engine-4 began treating the female sitting on the steps. As I walked through the door, there was another female subject prone on the floor. She was kind of crunched up against the wall with a large pool of blood under her head and chest. Her skin was extremely ashen and there was no movement. It was fairly easy to see this was not going to have a good outcome. I advised the officer that I needed to turn her over to assess the injury, and I did. She was obviously "Black" in the triage realm. She had a thru-and-thru gunshot wound (GSW) to the head with grey matter protruding from the apparent exit wound. This I deemed a mortal injury. I continued to the next subject. This young lady was sitting bolt upright with a perfectly round hole in the center of her forehead. She had agonal respirations, more commonly known on the streets as "fish breathing," and had a carotid as well as a radial pule. This scenario does not normally have a positive outcome, but assets were available, so we gave it our best shot. No pun intended. Well, there you go…time to go to work. I had the officer and other medic assist me in moving the patient to the floor as I keyed my mic and requested another medic unit to respond. The unit on scene would transport the "Red" patient with the GSW to the forehead, and the second responding unit would follow with the "Green" patient on the steps. The "Black" decedent would have to be handled by the medical examiner's office. The police would notify the Office of the Chief Medical Examiner (OCME) by phone, and an investigator would then respond to the scene, do their thing, and transport the body to the morgue for autopsy.

If one keeps everything in a manageable order, the calls normally flow smoothly. It is unfortunately easy to let that order slip away. I think if I denied that, I would be lying.

As Medic-4 started off to the emergency department, I advised the trauma center's medical communications (Med-Com) officer that Medic-4 was en route to their facility with an approximately 25-year-old black female who had suffered a GSW, thought to be a 9 mm, to the head. The entrance wound was to the center of the forehead and no exit. The patient was not responsive and had agonal respirations and a weak carotid pulse. Blood pressure was estimated at 60 systolic, and this would be a "Gold Alert." A Gold Alert was the highest degree of deep shit they had.

That was basically all the information the hospital needed to prepare for that patient. I then advised that a second patient would be transported momentarily by Medic-1. The patient had a GSW to the neck with what appeared to be minor injury. The patient was alert and oriented, and Medic-1 would contact Med-Com during transport with further information.

Oddly enough as the call was winding down, we found out there was a fourth victim who had run down the street and had a friend take him to the hospital with a GSW to his abdomen. That meant one fewer patient care report to write…oh yeah. We transported two out of three with number four transported by friends to the hospital.

The result was that the lady on the steps did fine, the dead on arrival (DOA) went to the state morgue, and the lady with the hole in her forehead did not survive and ultimately accompanied the DOA. Later, we heard that the guy who had bolted eventually recovered. Another wonderful day in the neighborhood.

We never heard who shot the four people. We never do, unless later subpoenaed for court or maybe read it in the newspaper or on the TV.

INCIDENT SEVEN:
"MAN DOWN"

Cardiac arrest calls are common in the EMS community. Unfortunately, most do not come out with a happy ending—but then, a few actually do. One such call came into dispatch as a man down, not breathing, at an auto sales dealership.

It was a warm day in early September in the middle of the afternoon. A good number of customers were in the dealership as well as several employees. Luckily, a couple of those people had been trained in Cardiopulmonary Resuscitation (CPR) and were willing to assist their fellow man in need. The dispatcher gave the pertinent information on the radio: "Engine-8, Medic-8, RS-1 respond to 4289 Gravely Drive for a man down, Code Blue with CPR in progress." I was already out and about and marked en route. Engine-8 with a captain/EMT, a lieutenant/paramedic (LT/Medic), and two firefighter/EMTs also marked up, as did Medic-8 with two firefighter/paramedics.

As it would happen, we all arrived at approximately the same time. The two EMTs initially took over CPR from the bystanders while the two paramedics from Medic-8 began to assess the situation and assemble the appropriate equipment.

My job at this point was to find out what had happened prior to the man's collapse and if anyone knew him and/or had any information about his medical history.

As it turned out, no one knew him, so we had to start from scratch. I took the man's wallet from his pocket as I looked for any sign of a medical alert bracelet, necklace, or card. Once again, a dead end...slight pun intended.

One medic applied some "slime" onto the defibrillation paddles and performed a "quick look" (obtaining a brief EKG tracing through the paddles, prior to placing the EKG pads on the chest) as the other assembled an airway kit. A third medic popped open the drug box and set up an IV to have a way to administer any medication the man might require. The medic with the paddles stated, "We have coarse V-fib...Clear...CLEAR!" Everyone took their hands off the patient, and a "THUD" was heard as the man's body jerked from the shock. Then the medic at the patient's head checked for a pulse but there was none to be found. Again, "Clear...CLEAR!" Another "THUD" was heard, and the body once again jerked as his arms slightly flailed. Once again, a check for a carotid pulse—a short wait and then the medic with his fingers on the patient's neck remarked, "We have a pulse." Unfortunately, he was still not breathing and needed to be intubated so we could truly secure his airway.

Once again, my role at this point was still backup and support. We certainly had enough personnel on scene to handle a cardiac arrest. The other two medics were already actively working their patient and one of the EMTs was still ventilating the patient with a bag-valve mask and suctioning his airway. The LT/Medic from Engine-8 set up for an intubation, while I got on the radio with med-com to make them aware of the current situation and attempt to give them an ETA at the hospital.

Most of the medics in our system had been taught intubations from the beginning utilizing a laryngoscope with either a "Miller" (thin straight blade) or "Macintosh" (thicker curved blade). I had found that the "Wisconsin" (thick straight blade) gave me better visualization of the vocal cords and other intubation landmarks. Another plus was that I could sweep the tongue out of the way and keep it there.

The LT/Medic had to suction the patient's airway due to the large amount of fluid and the patient's apparent lunch. He inserted his laryngoscope with the light shining brightly into the man's throat with his left hand as he held the No. 8 endotracheal tube, loaded with a stylet, at the ready in his right hand. He pulled out, continued to suction, and tried again. Once again, he had to retreat.

He looked up at me and asked if I wanted to give it a go. I said sure, no worries. I unrolled my airway equipment and stepped in at that point to intubate the patient. I had found in the past, on numerous occasions when we had a difficult intubation, I would be able to secure the airway with my Wisconsin blades.

The patient had lost his stomach contents, and we had to suction several times in an attempt to keep his airway clear. I suctioned once again and tried to visualize the landmarks required to place the endotracheal tube in the correct position. I was unable to locate anything past the tongue due to the amount of vomit blocking my sight. Once again, I suctioned, and the more I suctioned it seemed the more the man had to offer. He was in dire need of high-flow oxygen; without it, everything was for naught. If we didn't act swiftly, this was going to turn out to be a practice session, and this guy's family would never see him walk through the door at home again. His heart rate had been fast post-defibrillation, but now it was slowing. He needed air. I tried once again to place the tube past the vocal cords and into the trachea but without success. How terrible it would be to revive his heart only to lose him from lack of a secured airway.

I had one other trick up my sleeve. I quickly assembled a transtracheal jet insufflation device. It consisted of a few very simple, yet effective, components. I attached a three-inch, twelve-gauge angiocath onto a 10-cc syringe and made ready the oxygen supply line that was attached to the insufflator. I inserted the needle into the patient's neck, through the cricothyroid membrane at the bottom portion of what is commonly known as the Adam's apple. I then slightly withdrew the plunger to make sure I was in the correct spot and then advanced the catheter into his trachea. At that point, the syringe was removed, and the device used to control the oxygen going into his lungs was attached to the cath. Then I depressed the trigger, and the oxygen inflated his lungs as his upper airway blew clear. Basically, it is a small air gun with a trigger that both allows a large flow of oxygen to pass and suddenly stops the flow when the trigger is released. The advantage in this situation is that it supplies the patient with the oxygen he requires and also assists in clearing out the upper airway.

With the device in place, I was pretty much stuck at the airway position. Shortly afterward, we got a good air exchange going, the patient's heart rate picked up, and he started to try to breathe on his own. Quite honestly, no matter how long one works this job, when one resuscitates another human being, the adrenaline starts to flow, and the anticipation of a successful code begins to creep into one's mind. We knew full well that the chances of this man returning home as a whole human being was frightfully low. (We are good at saving hearts, but saving a brain is a tad more difficult.)

This patient, it appeared, was going to refuse to die at this place on this day. His heartbeat became stronger and more rapid, and his respirations increased and were very productive. I maintained the airway and continued at this point to assist his respirations only as needed. While all of this was going on, the EMTs had made ready the stretcher, and the other medics on scene had injected the patient with a medication to calm the heart as it was going too fast and had several anomalies that required additional medications. The patient also became rather combative, which is not unusual for post-resuscitation, and he was given medication to help calm him down.

We were, by this point in time, en route to the emergency department and had notified them of our deeds as well as our ETA. I heard later that day that our patient actually became alert and oriented, and this 57-year-old was, it looked like, going to make it this time. Another one for the good guys.

INCIDENT EIGHT:
"THAT'S IT, THAT'S ALL I HAVE"

Paramedics encounter many situations in their jobs that most people have never seen. This story is about one instance I wish I hadn't experienced either.

It was another unremarkable day in the life until the tones rang out and the dispatcher said, "Engine-11, Medic-8, RS-1 respond to 755 River Road for a man trapped in a machine at Walker's Textile Mill." The location was about a five-minute emergency run for me. Engine-11, with a firefighter-EMT captain, a lieutenant, and two firefighter-EMTs on board was literally just around the corner. Not far behind was Medic-8, which consisted of an EMT, and a paramedic named K. Williams. Williams and I had worked together for many years, and she was one of the most seasoned medics in the department.

The momentary silence on the radio was broken by "Engine-11 arriving 755 River Road, Engine-11 assuming command." Shortly thereafter I heard, "Medic-8 on scene." I arrived a couple of minutes after Medic-8, walked into the factory, and found everyone standing around trying to figure out what to do. Medic-8's personnel had reached the patient and placed a non-rebreathing oxygen mask on the fifty-two-year-old man who was obviously in a lot of trouble.

The patient had been operating a large textile roller/puller. I believe the purpose of the machine was to separate the fibers of the raw material. It looked like a large roller that was covered with thousands of quarter inch-long, razor-sharp blades.

To my amazement, as I approached the opposite side of the roller, I could see what appeared to be the man's fingers and hand flattened and spread out on the lower part of the roller. Blood was obviously present, and I could hear the patient screaming in pain. I walked around to the patient's side of the massive roller, and to my horror the man's arm was caught up to his elbow with all those tiny blades digging and spreading his hand and arm as if they were just another piece of cloth. I asked the plant manager if the machine had been locked out, and he said that it had. "Electrical lockout" assures the machine cannot be energized.

The engine captain and I discussed with the plant manager if anyone was able to disassemble the machine. The answer was a big fat "NO." Not because they didn't want to, but they just didn't have the equipment or knowledge to take it apart without doing more damage to the man's arm. The patient by this time was going into shock and was in serious condition. We talked about re-energizing the machine in reverse, but that was not an option either. We discussed using airbags, the jaws of life, or anything else we could come up with, and nothing seemed to be able to solve the problem at hand...OK...maybe a little pun intended.

The man had been operating the roller and had luckily just shut down the power. The roller was almost stopped when it caught onto his shirt sleeve and pulled his arm into the monster's mouth. Apparently, had the machine been running full bore, it would not only have pulled in his arm but also his entire body.

Audie, the battalion chief on duty with our department, had arrived and been filled in on the unique situation. Audie had a vast amount of experience with heavy and tactical rescue, but this time none of us had a solution to our current predicament.

While all the conversations transpired, Paramedic Williams started an IV of Ringer's lactate on the man's other arm and placed a tourniquet on the affected arm at the brachial artery pressure point, a few inches above the elbow.

I called the hospital to advise them of the situation and how dire it was. I told the emergency department physician that the man needed to be removed from the machine and that we had run out of options, other than a field amputation. The doctor asked if I had the necessary equipment, and I replied that I could come up with something. I also advised that it appeared I could possibly get to the tissue that was smashed and cut the patient out with a scalpel. I stated the only option for cutting through the bone, if necessary, would be a hack saw. I also told him that all we had on scene to help sedate the patient were 20 mgs of morphine and 20 mgs of valium. I made it very clear that if they wanted to send someone to us to perform the procedure, I certainly had no problem with that. I was told flatly there was no one to send, to go ahead with the procedure, and to advise when we were en route to the emergency department.

To gain access to the patient, I would have to drape my body over the roller. I had one of the firefighters hand me a large rubber mat from the factory floor, and I draped it over the roller as to not place my chest and abdomen directly on the blades. I had Paramedic Williams get a scalpel from the obstetrics kit on her unit, and one of the factory workers gave me a five-inch mirror. Unfortunately, I could just barely see where the arm met the angry little blades. I had to use the mirror to really see what I was doing. Below is a photo of the side of the machine.

So, picture this: I am upside down inside this huge machine with this poor guy who is still conscious. Bob Watkins was his name. I introduced myself and said, "Mr. Watkins, you know what I'm going to have to do, right?" He replied fairly calmly, "Yes, just give me everything you can and do it as fast as you can. I knew when I got caught in that damn thing what was going to happen."

He had resigned himself to the fact that he was losing his arm, so I proceeded. I put on a pair of surgical gloves and directed Paramedic Williams to administer the morphine, titrating to his level of consciousness (LOC). As the patient seemed to relax a bit, I started to cut the tissue as close to the blades as possible so I could save as much of his arm as I could while still freeing this poor guy from that massive beast. I'm not sure how much time it took to get to the bone, but if felt like an eternity. It was very hot inside the factory, and between the sweat and trying to see what I was doing with the blood-soaked mirror…well, let's put it this way: I had had better days, and I'm sure, so had my patient. As the bleeding got a bit worse, Paramedic Williams tightened the tourniquet. She stayed right beside me throughout the entire incident and handled everything very professionally. Several of the firefighters, however, had trouble watching.

I cut all the way around the patient's arm, and to my dismay, I still had solid bone to remove I remember looking at Audie and asking him to get someone to obtain a hack saw from Engine-11 and do everything they could to sterilize the blade. I heard someone exclaim, "He needs what?" The engine captain got one of their hack saws and a propane torch along with a bottle of alcohol from the ambulance. They heated the blade and, after it had cooled a bit, doused it in alcohol. This was pretty much the best they could do.

I had already cut my gloves several times along with my knuckles as I attempted to slice with the scalpel as close to the tiny blades as possible. I gloved up again before grabbing the hack saw, and then I tried to cut into the bone. Paramedic Williams administered another 10 mgs of morphine, and the patient once again relaxed a bit but remained conscious. Next would be the valium since that was all we had left. Utilizing hindsight, I should have called for another medic unit to obtain another drug box, with additional morphine.

The hack saw was just too bulky for me to get as close to the roller as I needed, so I took the blade off the saw handle and used the blade by itself.

If you have ever gone deer hunting and had to cut through a large leg bone, then you have some idea what I had to do to get this man to freedom and into definitive care. By this time, all the valium had been administered but he was still alert and oriented. Such a strong-willed man indeed.

With every stroke of the saw blade, I felt my knuckles dragging over the tiny razor blades. Mr. Watkins would occasionally give out a scream due to what I am sure was excruciating pain.

I looked at him and asked, "Do you like to go fishing?" He quickly replied, "I sure as hell do!" The conversation continued, "Do you fish for stripers, largemouth, catfish, or what? He said, "Catfish are my favorite."

50

I'm not sure how long I was able to keep him thinking about fishing, but it was at least a short diversion from the horror we were both facing.

Eventually, changing gloves became a joke and we accepted the fact that Bob and I were clearly blood brothers by that point.

The sawing back and forth continued for several minutes that quite frankly felt like several hours. Mr. Watkins remained conscious throughout his horrific ordeal, and we continued to discuss hobbies and family. I have no idea how he endured the pain and knowledge of what was happening to him. Finally, we freed our patient from his confinement, and I looked over at Paramedic Williams and simply told her that I was done, and he was her patient. I remember telling her, "That's it, that's all I have."

I honestly don't know if I have ever been so physically and emotionally exhausted in my life. Being an avid cigarette smoker back in the day, I recall walking over to a sink, cleaning off the blood that covered my arms, and lighting and consuming several smokes back-to-back. Audie told me later that the ED physician wanted him to place the amputated arm in a clean sheet and bring it to the hospital. Audie said he explained to them that the severed part of the man's arm was literally mush inside the machine's roller. There was nothing to transport to the hospital

I came home that next morning, called to my wife, and exclaimed, "You are not going to believe what I had to do at work." Knowing how nuts some of the stories had been in the past, she said, "What now?" I damn near cried and just mumbled out, "I had to cut a man's arm off." She just looked at me in disbelief and hugged me. That was a well-needed hug.

The next day, I went to the hospital and dropped in on my former patient. I really felt the need to apologize. I remember saying something like, "Sir, I hope you are doing well, and I am so sorry I had to take off your arm." He looked me dead in the eye and said, "Thank you for getting me out of that damn mess and saving my life." That is a comment that paramedics don't get to hear very often. We made additional small talk about fishing again, and shortly after, I left his hospital room with a mixed bag of sorrow and accomplishment. I never saw Bob Watkins again, but I heard he did...well...OK.

INCIDENT NINE:
"18ᵀᴴ STREET, MULTIPLE VICTIMS"

After eighteen hours of a twenty-four-hour shift had past, the lights blared on, the loud, annoying tone rung out, and a kind voice calmly stated, "Engine-9, Medic-9, RS-1 respond to 1800 block of Primrose Street Northwest for four to five shots heard, subject down." She repeated the information as all who had been alerted were already on the way to their respective apparatus bays to man the requested equipment.

In this incident, Engine-9 consisted of a captain/EMT, a lieutenant/paramedic, and two firefighter/EMTs. Medic-9 had two firefighter/paramedics on board. Both units were housed together and happened to be near the scene itself. I, on the other hand, was stationed on the opposite side of the city and had a bit further to travel. E-9's Captain marked up on the radio and stated, "Engine-9 and Medic-9 both en route as well as standing by for PD (the police)." I simply marked en route.

Just a small reminder: when responding to a call that obviously involves violence such as shootings, stabbings, or armed robberies, our protocol was to hold back at a safe location near the scene. We would maintain our position until the scene was deemed safe by the police. This worked most of the time, but it was not a slam dunk. The police could do only so much when the scene was widespread, which was the case in this situation.

A police officer on scene reported back to the dispatcher that the scene was secure and for Fire-EMS to come in. The next communication from the officer was rather chilling, as he said, "Tell EMS to hurry! Multiple victims, multiple victims!"

In general, men and women who work on the streets with the police department, the fire department, and EMS do not get overly excited on the radio unless something is super bad or is totally out of their control. In this instance, the police officer apparently was looking at a scene that was spread over an entire city block and had more subjects down than even he was aware.

Prior to my arrival, I put out a request for an additional medic unit to respond due to the initial report from the police officer. Engine-9 and Medic-9 marked on scene, and police immediately drew them into initiating patient care, directing them to different patients from one end of the block to the other.

Dispatch, once again, sounded out on the radio and advised that they had at least three gunshot victims, and I immediately requested a third medic unit to respond. Upon my arrival, a large number of police cars blocked the street to the point I had to exit my vehicle at least a half of a block from the scene. Medic-9 and Engine-9's personnel were all on the other side of the scene and very busy.

As I approached, I found one victim on the side of the street with a police officer attending to the patient's leg wound. I quickly assessed the situation and requested that the officer stay with the patient for the time being. He agreed, and I asked if he knew how many victims we had. He said, "Several, maybe six to eight."

I got back on the radio and requested one more medic unit and an engine company to respond, and I assumed command of the scene. I walked through and triaged the patients as I came to them and made assignments either face-to-face or on the radio.

By this time, Engine-4, Medic-4 were en route with four additional EMTs and three more medics.

Determining how many units are necessary to handle any given scene depends on the number and condition of the patients. Also, if you remember from a previous incident in this book, triage has four basic levels. This scene would require utilization of all four of the triage categories. Additional unit assignments were made either on or prior to arrival on the scene.

Triage went as follows:

Patient No. 1: GSW to the leg (Green-minor), walking wounded or can wait for transport.

Patient No. 2: GSW to the arm (Green-minor), walking wounded or can wait for transport.

At this point, I requested that Medic-1 also respond to the scene, which, due to additional ongoing calls, depleted our medic unit resources. A request was then made to have a mutual aid call go out for medic units to stand-by for the city.

We were blessed with a county system that had very capable medical personnel, and the local trauma center had their own Advanced Life Support units that could be made available. We also had quite a few medical personnel on engine and ladder companies all over the city to assist in any other immediate needs.

Patient No. 3: GSWs to the buttocks, arm, and leg ("Yellow"-delayed); stable vitals, serious but not life-threating injuries, transport prior to "Green" patients. Trauma Alert at emergency department.

Patient No. 4: GSWs to right flank and left flank ("Red"-immediate); unstable vitals, considered life-threating injuries, priority transport. Gold Alert at emergency department.

Patient No. 5, GSWs to upper left abdomen and lower right abdomen ("Red"-immediate); unstable vitals, considered life-threating injuries, priority transport. Gold Alert at emergency department.

Patient No. 6, GSW to chest ("Black"-DOA); Subject deceased, transport not required, handled by medical examiner's office.

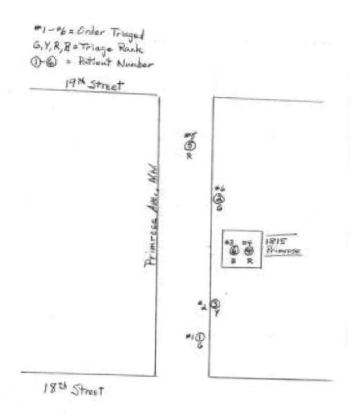

So, with that said, we had several patients that needed treatment and transportation to the hospital and one decedent that did not.

At 3:21 a.m., Medic-9 continued treatment and transported patient No. 4 (Gold Alert) to the trauma center emergency department

At 3:22 a.m., Medic-6 continued treatment and transported patient No. 5 (Gold Alert) to the trauma center emergency department

At 3:26 a.m., Medic-4 continued treatment and transported patient No. 3 (Trauma Alert) to the trauma center emergency department

At 3:34 a.m., Medic-1 treated and transported patients Nos. 1 and 2 to the trauma center emergency department

I notified the medical communications (Med-Com) officer at the trauma center early in the incident that we had multiple gunshot victims with several different degrees of injury. After the first unit departed the scene, I advised the emergency department/Med-Com of each unit's ETA to the ED and the severity of their patients.

In total, we had about thirty police officers, several detectives, and sixteen fire-EMS personnel on scene. We also had a mutual aid unit and pretty much everyone else on standby for the city. This entire call for fire-EMS lasted approximately thirty-nine minutes from the time the call rang out to the time the last patient was transported. A lot to be said for all involved, job well done.

INCIDENT TEN:
"TWO DOWN, WEAPONS OUT, NIP JOINT"

Early in the life of the city's Emergency Medical Services Department— and prior to its merger with the fire department—the protocols for responding to different types of incidents were not really set—at least, not set in stone.

We received a call for a police raid on a "nip joint" where illegal gambling was occurring and drugs were normally in use, with two subjects down inside. As the EMS Supervisor, it was part of my responsibility to decide when to enter a scene or not. I responded, as did Medic-4 and Medic-1. I radioed Medic-4, as they would arrive first, and told them to stand by until we got a better picture of what was going down. Once the police told us through dispatch that the scene was safe, we proceeded. I went in first to find a large number of police cars blocking any hope of driving up to the house in question. I exited my vehicle, as did the medics, and I had them hold back for a few moments as I approached.

When I saw the first officer, his eyes were wide, and he appeared on alert with his pistol drawn and aimed to the sky. His finger was on the outside of the trigger guard, ready and waiting. I asked what was going on, and he said they had two subjects who had exchanged fire with the officers and had been shot. The suspects were both in the house, and they needed immediate assistance. I asked if the scene was secure, and he said, "As secure as it's going to get. There are a lot of weapons in and around the house and they don't all belong to PD." I heard another officer yell for me to hurry. I advanced to the house to see several officers with their pistols out guarding the front door, and I advised the medics to bring stretchers only. This was obviously going to be a rapid rescue rather than the typical "treat and transport."

There were civilians walking around the outside of the house as well as several still inside. Some had their hands behind their backs with metal bracelets applied. Others were just standing and looking at the men bleeding on the floor.

One police sergeant estimated there had been seventy-five to one-hundred people in the house when the police barged into the front and back doors at the same time. There were simply too many people for the police to control.

I advised the medics to grab-and-go, no on-scene treatment. We had encountered similar incidents in the past where rescue of a patient was first and foremost due to the lack of stability of the scene itself. This was handled by extricating the patients from the scene, driving several blocks, and then initiating treatment. My personnel had to be kept safe or we would not be able to properly treat the patients.

In the mid to late '80s, the city issued bulletproof vests to the medics. They also replaced the windows in one of the EMS stations with bulletproof glass. This was really a joke as it was a cinderblock building; the only safe place was behind the windows. In my first station, it was not unusual to hear gunfire during the night. We would hear it and say something like, "I guess that's our next customer." And sometimes it was.

I suppose I should get back to the story at hand. The medics did indeed drive several blocks so as not to stay in the line of fire, assessed the patients, and initiated treatment. The rest was taken care of en route to the hospital. In those days, a severe GSW patient would have their wound or wounds covered in an attempt to control bleeding. Then we would administer high-flow oxygen and insert a couple of large-bore IVs flowing with Ringer's lactate solution into the patient. Many times, Military Anti-Shock Trousers (MAST) would also be put in place as a prophylactic measure. If the patient went into shock, we would inflate the MAST and bring his or her blood pressure back up. So many discoveries and protocol changes over the years have improved treatment of this type of patient.

(Sidebar: You newbies out there have probably only seen MAST in a museum. It used to be a thing.)

I had already advised the trauma center that we had two units en route. One patient had a gunshot wound to the leg that apparently struck the femoral artery, and the other patient had a gunshot wound to the abdomen. Police had found 9 mm and .38-caliber casings at the scene. Both patients were considered "Red" within the triage realm, and my calling ahead took that responsibility off the backs of the medics. They were busy enough trying to treat the patients. Calling ahead also warned the hospital of the upcoming onslaught. Quite often after any type of shooting, many people—either family, friends, or foes—will go to the emergency department and cause havoc. After several years of this, the hospitals learned to lockdown the emergency department and allow only EMS personnel and patients inside.

Oh well…another wonderful day (night) in the neighborhood.

INCIDENT ELEVEN:
"THE HOSTAGE TAKER"

Shots fired; shots fired!!!…Hit the deck!!!

With that said, I'm going to set the stage for this incident before we go any further. It was late one afternoon around dusk when a man armed with a rifle walked into a small diner where his girlfriend was eating. He held her at gunpoint, and someone outside the diner called 9-1-1. I really don't know what beef he had with his girlfriend, nor do I care, and quite frankly, at this point it doesn't really matter.

The police responded appropriately with several units and contacted the hostage taker via a telephone inside the diner. A conversation ensued that lasted for several hours. During that time, many officers made their way to the scene. The dispatcher notified me by phone that they had a hostage situation and then dispatched me, the EMS operations captain, along with a medic unit consisting of two paramedics, to stand by just in case. We responded silently and took up a position about a block from the scene.

Upon our arrival, we saw approximately ten police cars and several unmarked cars and officers to match, but no one had blocked the road leading up to the active crime scene. I pulled my response vehicle, a Chevy 2500 pickup truck decked out in red-and-white rapidly flashing strobe lights, across the road and blocked it. I advised dispatch that I had the road secured and would continue to stand by at that location. With my new parking spot, approximately a half a block closer than the original, I had a little better view of the ongoing hostage scene. I could see probably twenty or so police officers with pistols drawn and to the ready holding cover behind their black-and-white cruisers with bright blue strobe lights flashing. I noted several long guns out as well. I was not privy to the conversation being carried out with the armed

POPE

subject, but the officers would occasionally seem a bit more relaxed and then tense up and appear to be more "on guard."

Time was passing and not much was really going on from my vantage point. I was standing behind my vehicle with the crime scene in view, just watching and continuing to turn sightseers around as they wandered up to my location.

All of the sudden, the young woman who had been the subject of the hostage taking walked out of the diner along with five other occupants, leaving only the perpetrator inside. Whoever had been negotiating had apparently been productive.

The young man, still in the diner, then turned the rifle on himself and threatened to pull the trigger. Being good guys with guns, the police did not want him to succeed with his thoughts, so they continued to try to talk him down from his self-imposed perch.

Everything had been quiet for a couple of more hours or more, and by then the total incident had been ongoing for approximately five hours.

Suddenly, I noticed massive movement on the part of the officers as the young man walked out of the diner, still with the rifle pointed at himself. He calmly walked across the street as the police parted, reminiscent of the Red Sea. He made his way to a small grassy area next to a business. He was standing in front of a two-story cinderblock wall, and his new position had taken him just outside of my direct view, which I thought was a good thing at the time. Shortly thereafter, I saw a city utility truck pull in with light stands, which they set up and aimed toward the area occupied by the perpetrator.

The standoff continued for at least another hour before the police lieutenant on scene, who was in charge, walked toward the subject, bull horn in hand, and continued asking him to put down his weapon and surrender to the police. I'm not sure how many times I heard, "Put the gun down." I'm positive at least a hundred.

A few more minutes passed and then, as if several people had lit off a large number of firecrackers and cherry bombs, all I could hear was "POP, POP, POP, POP, BOOM, POP, POP, BOOM, POP" and so on and so on. I'm sure it didn't last too long, but it seemed to go on forever.

As soon as the melee started, I hit the deck. I couldn't tell for sure where all the gunfire was coming from. Right before I heard the first POPs and BOOMs, I saw most of the officers with their weapons pointed toward where I understood the perpetrator to be standing, although he was still out of my line of sight.

This I swear is true: I don't remember ever cursing or for that matter saying anything off-color on the radio, but when the dispatcher called me and said, "Shots fired, shots fired," I reached for my mic button, depressed it, and said, "NO SHIT!"

Well, anytime there is a hail of bullets someone is generally going to get hurt. My concern was, with all the shooting, I would run around the corner to find several police officers, many of which were my friends, shot along with the gunman.

The next thing I heard on the radio, as well as from some of the officers yelling, was MEDIC, MEDIC!!!! The next thought that went through my mind was, "I guess it's my turn." I radioed the medic unit that was standing by to come on in as I rounded the corner of the building to several visual and olfactory clues. Gun smoke was in the air, as was dust from the side of the building. The lights from the light stands were bright. Several officers were waving at me to continue toward them where I found only one subject down to my pleasant surprise. It was the gunman. He was flat on his back on the ground, so I started to assess his injuries as I asked if anyone else was hurt. The answer was a resounding no.

I started counting the number of gunshot wounds I considered mortal injuries. The count went like this: one, two, three, four, five, six in the chest and one, two, three in the head. The subject was still taking agonal respirations, which I had seen many times before, and I recognized that he was not going to survive the amount of lead his body had just absorbed. One officer came up to me and said, "Help him! Do what you can to save him!" My answer was something like, "The only piece of equipment I need is a sheet. Y'all took care of everything else. He'll quit that shit in a few seconds"—which he did. That might have been crass, but it was honest. I did not mean or intend any disrespect for the officers; I was only answering their request for assistance with an honest reply. One of the other medics obtained a white sheet from the ambulance and covered the deceased gunman.

I walked over to a young officer who appeared to be rather distraught and asked if I could assist in any way. He simply looked at me with a horror-stricken look on his face and said, "I think I hit him in the head, and I just kept shooting. I couldn't stop." My understanding was that he unloaded the magazine in his .40-caliber Glock, which consisted of fifteen rounds. He also said that the gunman had raised his rifle toward the lieutenant who was trying to talk him down, and when he did that, all hell broke loose. I believe many of the officers on the scene discharged their weapons, including at least one or two of the twelve-gauge shotguns that were aimed in the direction of the young man now lying under the sheet on the ground.

Last I heard, there were between forty and fifty rounds discharged on that scene. I didn't and still don't blame any of the officers. They did everything within their power at the time to avoid hurting that young man. It just didn't work out the way they had wished or intended.

I went back to the scene the next day so I could see everything in the daylight. The diner, a section of the road, and the grassy area were still blocked off with bright yellow crime scene tape. The police forensic officers were doing their thing as well. I looked at that cinderblock wall, and, not to my surprise, I saw a great number of bullet holes and marks. What did surprise me was that there were quite a few marks that appeared to be bullet holes rather high on the wall. I also noticed a couple of patterns that resembled buck shot from a twelve-gauge shotgun about fifteen to twenty feet up the wall. I thought that was a bit unusual and wondered just how the officers were aiming the shotguns. Interesting, I would say, at the very least.

I never did talk to that unnerved young officer again about that shooting, but I'm sure that affected him for the rest of his life.

I was called into the detective's office to give a statement a couple of days later. The detective asked me what I saw and heard prior to the shooting, and I told him pretty much the same thing I have described here. Then he asked what I saw and heard after the shooting began. I smiled at the detective and said, "The only thing I heard was a large number of gunshots and the only thing I saw was Goodyear and pavement." He kind of sat back in his fake-leather roller chair and smiled back at me. I told him I got as intimate with the pavement as I could because I had no idea in which direction all the gunfire was going. That pretty much ended that interview.

Note: remember the approximate number of shots fired on this scene; it will come back into play in the following incident. Also be advised that the Tactical Response Team (TRT) was available at the time of the hostage-taking but was not requested.

INCIDENT TWELVE:
"GET HIM...GET THAT SOB!"

"That's him! Get that M***** F*****! Get him, get that son of a bitch!"

Once again, I need to set up the scene so that you, the reader, will understand the previous expletives. It was a rather warm, clear evening, if memory serves. We received a call to assist police at the scene of a shooting. Medic-4 and I, in RS-1, responded, and prior to our arrival, police requested that only one paramedic come in. We all knew what that meant. They didn't want several people unnecessarily traipsing around the crime scene. They just needed one medic to enter, pronounce the person dead, and leave. Since I was responding that job fell on my shoulders. I advised Medic-4 to stand by at the bottom of the hill, leading up to the scene. As I drove by, I gave them a nod with a wave, and as I approached the scene, I noted approximately four or five police cars and a couple of unmarked detective vehicles. I advised the dispatcher that I had arrived on scene.

This incident occurred in a low-rent housing (Section Eight) complex. There were probably fifteen or twenty apartment buildings in the complex, and it looked like everyone that lived there had emptied out into street. I was met at the front of the building by a uniformed officer and a detective. We all knew each other because we had been through this drill many times before. We greeted one another, and my next question was, "What do we have?" The detective said, "I just need you to carefully walk through the scene and check the two women who are down and then exit the scene."

In past situations like this, I would put on gloves and be very careful where I stepped so as not to interfere with any possible evidence. I would then make sure I walked out using the same path I took to enter the scene.

This was no exception. I approached the first subject, who was supine on the floor in a common hallway of the apartment building and observed a female with a large wound to her left temple. There was a considerable amount of blood on the floor, and I checked for a carotid pulse and there was none. I took a quick listen with a stethoscope for lung sounds or heartbeats and there were none. I advised the detective that subject No. 1 was deceased, and he took me to the second female inside the apartment, also on the floor. I checked subject No. 2 in similar fashion and the same result was found. I also noted what appeared to be several 9 mm brass casings on the floor of the apartment as well as in the hallway. I wrote down the pertinent information about the victims, such as name, age, etc. I documented my findings on a notepad and exited the crime scene. I also jotted down a brief diagram of the location of the bodies.

I have found in the past that it is wise to put as much information to paper prior to leaving the scene. This will help if I am subpoenaed a year or two later. One's memory is only so dependable, especially when encountering a large quantity of calls. I walked outside and advised Medic-4 that they could clear the scene and that I would handle the paperwork.

I then walked over to my vehicle, sat down, and started compiling the information I had obtained in the house onto an official EMS run report.

I had almost completed writing the report when I noticed a close friend of mine, who happened to be a police sergeant, standing nearby. I walked over to say hi, and we engaged in a brief conversation. I was about to return to my vehicle to leave the scene—keep in mind, there are probably a couple hundred people standing around on the street and in the parking lots of the buildings—when a man waving a pistol in the air ran around from the corner of the building where my friend and I were standing. A lady standing nearby screamed at the top of her lungs, "That's him! Get that M***** F*****! Get him, get that son of a bitch!" I might add that was one hell of a surprise.

The gunman ran through the crowed street. My friend ran in pursuit. Apparently, the word had spread rather fast, and, of course, the sergeant got on his radio and alerted all the other officers. The armed subject encountered another officer as he ran, and they engaged in a hand-to-hand conflict.

I'm going to back up for just a moment. Not only were there a multitude of civilians on the street but the media had also responded in force after hearing of a double homicide. It was dark by this time, and the lights from several media video cameras as well as camera flashes lit up the scene as if it were daylight.

Back to the fight. It was surreal to see that officer with his pistol drawn and the gunman with his weapon in hand fist-fighting and wrestling on the ground. The bad guy with a gun got the best of the good guy and ran off, thank God, rather than shooting the officer or anyone else. The suspect ran to a place where two of the buildings came together and formed an impenetrable barrier. At this point, the police started herding the public back and away from the new scene and holding the subject at bay. The gunman then held the pistol to his own head and a stalemate began.

By this time, many additional police officers had arrived, as well as a tactical response team (TRT). They set up an attempt at negotiations and determined the subject was now "in containment." They had a sniper set up camp, and I was able to listen in on most of the police radio traffic. I also had dispatch call Medic-4 to return to the scene, work their way up the hill, and stand by.

My vehicle was blocked in by the onslaught of police cars; I was stuck regardless of how this turned out. The standoff continued for at least another hour when...remember when I told you not to forget the little thing about forty to fifty rounds going off in the last incident? Well, this is where that enters the conversation. Picture this: I was standing behind my vehicle about fifty yards away from the active scene and could not see the suspect holding the pistol. He was hidden by one of the buildings. I could see a large group of people between me and the scene, as well as the officers maintaining "containment."

OK, here we go—the bad guy with a gun walked out of "containment" through the crowd and started to run in my direction. The sniper didn't shoot, nor did the other officers. So, I was looking at this crazy gunman running toward me with about twenty police officers and detectives with their weapons drawn and pointed directly at his back and my face. I am literally looking down their gun barrels!

Flash back to the previous incident with the hostage situation, which turned into a threatened suicide, which turned into a DOA. Once again, the next thing I became intimate with was that familiar Goodyear insignia, and I initiated an extremely close inspection of the asphalt. My next thought was that there may be either a hail of bullets coming my way, or the gunman might even choose to hide with me. I did not particularly like the thought of either outcome.

As it turned out, the bad guy with the gun turned and ran between two of the complex's buildings and the officers pursued. Within just a few minutes, I heard a single "POP." I thought, really? That's it? Only one shot? Thank God!

And then, an all-too-familiar sound coming from the direction of the gunshot—Medic! Need a Medic! Once again, it was my turn. Medic-4's personnel and I approached the then-unarmed subject on the ground with an apparent gunshot wound to his abdomen. We worked a bit on the man and made him ready for transport. Medic-4 transported him to the trauma center as a Gold Alert, a serious trauma patient. I cleared the scene, happy that this one was over. I heard later that the gunman did rather well and would stand trial for the double homicide. I was subpoenaed and testified with my two cents' worth in the case, and the man was in fact convicted of killing both women. I understand he served only sixteen years.

INCIDENT THIRTEEN:
"ODORLESS AND COLORLESS GAS"

Carbon monoxide (CO) is an odorless and colorless gas and can be deadly. CO is produced by the incomplete combustion of many different materials. It is also slightly lighter than air and diffuses evenly throughout a room or building. This incident involves a malfunctioning natural gas furnace leaking CO in the basement of a home. The home was occupied by four people. They were all fast asleep, and then something went terribly wrong.

We received the call at approximately eight-thirty that morning. The tones rang out at the respective stations and the dispatcher called out, "Engine-9, Medic-9, Ladder-2, Battalion Chief-2, RS-1…Respond to 544 Madden Street Northwest for the report of four subjects down in a home. Unknown reason. Caller states cannot wake the subjects."

Our response consisted of an engine company with four firefighter-EMT's on board, a ladder company also with four personnel, three firefighter-EMT's and a paramedic, a medic unit with two medics, a battalion chief and an EMS captain. The tones blared out a second time and after the dispatcher's second announcement, I requested a second medic unit to be dispatched. Medic-2 was dispatched within moments. Engine-5 arrived on scene first and attempted to contact the occupants. The person who called 9-1-1 apparently was a friend who came in and found the people.

The engine captain made entry and found two men and a woman down on the floor and one woman walking around in a daze. At first, we really didn't know for sure what had happened, but it became rapidly apparent that this was a CO poisoning. The lieutenant from Ladder 2 checked the house with a CO monitor, and the level was extremely high.

First things first, we removed the patients from the toxic environment and initiated treatment outside. We had one male in full cardiac arrest and two other subjects, a male and a female, who had pulses but were trying to breathe through a mass of foam that had accumulated on their faces. They both had massive pulmonary edema and were in respiratory arrest. Shortly after my arrival on scene, a third medic unit was requested, and Medic-1 was quickly dispatched. Because all the fire-EMS personnel were at least EMTs and several of the personnel responding on the fire apparatus were paramedics, the manpower was more than sufficient to handle the call.

Carbon monoxide binds very strongly to the iron in the hemoglobin in the blood. Once CO attaches, it is very difficult to release. So, if you breathe in carbon monoxide, it sticks to your hemoglobin and takes up all the oxygen binding sites. Your blood loses its ability to transport oxygen and you suffocate.

Because CO binds to hemoglobin so strongly, you can be poisoned by CO even at very low concentrations if you are exposed for a long period of time. Concentrations as low as twenty or thirty parts per million (PPM) can be harmful if you are exposed for several hours. Exposure at two-thousand PPM for one hour will cause unconsciousness.

Many common devices produce carbon monoxide, including gasoline engines, natural gas and propane appliances, wood and coal stoves, especially if used in a confined space.

The male patient in respiratory arrest was worked on at the scene, but ultimately declared DOA. The other man who was down and in respiratory arrest when we arrived was intubated, treated, and transported to the emergency department. After several days in the hospital, he walked out. The third patient also did well after several days in the hospital, and the lady who was walking around recovered rapidly after being removed from the poisonous gas. She was also transported and spent at least a night in the hospital prior to being discharged.

The friend, in this case, was the hero. If he had not gone in, found them and alerted 9-1-1, the outcome would have been extremely grim.

One thing was missing in this home—a CO detector. Just like a smoke detector with a fire, a CO detector would have set off an alarm and probably saved the life that was lost and prevented this terrible event from the start. Just a word to the wise.

INCIDENT FOURTEEN:
"MIDNIGHT RIDE"

I had been working with the medical examiner's office for a couple of years, and after thirty years as a paramedic, trying to save people, the last two years with the ME's office were oddly calming. There was literally nothing I could do that would kill a client. I had been designated a diplomate by the American Board of Medicolegal Death Investigators, also known as a D-ABMDI. What a mouthful that is. Basically, what this means is that I had actively worked as an investigator with the ME's office for at least two years. I also had learned how to do really gross stuff to dead people, as well as having passed a rather grueling four-hour test on a computer with a state monitor standing right behind me, watching every twitch I made.

So much for qualifications. I worked midnights in the morgue. We had offices in the front of the building and autopsy suites in the back, along with a couple of coolers. One cooler was much larger than the other one. The smaller cooler had lockable cages, and it was known as the intake cooler and held about five bodies The larger one held approximately twenty or more, depending on how you placed them.

The first thing we did upon arriving to work was to get a turnover, or status report, from the investigator going off duty. Once the turnover was complete, I was normally the only person, who could talk remaining in the building. Then the fun started.

I always looked at the reports and then walked back to the large cooler to count the bodies. Generally, there would be anywhere from two to ten, depending on how the day had gone for the general population of the thirty-four counties for which our office was responsible. The powers that be didn't like it when the numbers in the reports didn't match the number of decedents. Can't say I blamed them. Not that that ever happened. Then I marched on to the intake cooler. Sometimes it would be completely full and then other times empty. After that, I settled into my office chair and started working on the endless files of decedents on my desk.

One night, after working for a few hours, I received a phone call from a state trooper requesting my presence at an airplane crash a couple of counties away. I asked him a number of pointed questions and began filling out an intake form. After about fifteen minutes or so, I started to load up my investigator "stuff" and head out the door. Then I remembered we had a new pathologist in training, and I called her to see if she would like to go on a road trip for a plane flying into the side of a mountain. She sounded excited—I suppose because she had never seen a real plane crash— so the answer was an exuberant "yes."

I waited only about fifteen minutes for her to arrive. She came in with her brand new, freshly pressed, spanking clean jump suit as well as her new helmet with the Office of the Chief Medical Officer (OCME) sticker on the front. She also had in her hand a jump kit that had been pre-assembled by one of the other pathologists, and we started on our merry way.

I know you have all heard stories, both true and fictional, that start with, "It was a dark and stormy night." Well, it *was* a dark and stormy night. We had about an hour's drive into a very rural county, and the flashes of lightning were the only things other than our weak headlights showing the way. I had some knowledge of the area and felt comfortable making it there and back. But I kind of let on to the young doctor that I was lost. My anxious passenger was not too terribly amused. Hey, if you can't have some fun working midnights at the morgue, then what?

Our hour-long drive turned into about an hour and a half due to the inclement weather conditions, and one of the waiting troopers called to make sure we were still on the way. Shortly thereafter, we arrived to find a state police car with blue lights flashing and blocking a small dirt road. We pulled up to the car and the trooper exited, putting on his rain gear and plastic-covered wide brim hat and walked over to the driver's side window. We had a magnetic sign, on the side of the van, that our office used for just this type of occasion with the official name of the organization clear to see. When we wished to be more discreet, the sign stayed inside the vehicle. The trooper asked to see our identifications, and we produced our badges as well as IDs. He kindly allowed us to pass and gave brief directions. We had to drive another five or six hundred yards on a winding dirt road, with tall trees on both sides of the road, to find another police car with one trooper inside. It was still raining cats and dogs, so we all donned our rain gear, and the trooper began to lead us to the scene where he had set up a couple of flood lights.

As we approached the site of the crash, you could see where the trees had been sheared. First the tops of the trees were gone and then, we noticed, the trees were marked up and bent over a bit further down the trunks. The smell of avgas, the type of fuel used in most small aircraft, was very strong as were the different smells associated with the burning of wood and rubber. However, there were no active fires. This was the same trooper I had spoken to on the phone earlier, and he had assured me that we would be able to safely conduct our scene investigation as well as retrieve the decedent.

We finally approached the crumpled, twisted, gnarly mess that was left of the twin-engine aircraft. That ill-fated pilot, after crunching through the trees, probably last saw the rock face just prior to making contact, with all the mighty force of the engines and gravity to assist.

We had also been informed earlier that only one person, the pilot, had been occupying the plane. The doctor and I looked around with our flashlights, being careful not to step on any evidence that might help the National Transportation and Safety Board (NTSB) discover the cause of the crash and the demise of the lost soul. I took several photographs, documenting what I was shooting as well as the location in reference to a grid the police had already set up. After several minutes at the ultimate resting place of the aircraft, I asked the trooper exactly where the decedent was located, and he stated rather succinctly, "Oh, he is still in the cockpit." My follow-up was, "OK, where is the cockpit?" He did not direct me to something I could really identify as an airplane cockpit nor were we able to locate the decedent. The officer said, "Well, he's right there." I had a private conversation with my new friend, the doctor, and advised her that the trip had been for naught. There was no way we were going to be able to find all the pieces and parts that we would need to take back to the office for identification of the decedent.

I will be no more graphic out of respect for the decedent and the family in case they read this and are able to figure out of whom I speak. Because it was extremely dark and we had only a couple of flashlights and very little assistance, I turned to the trooper and advised him that we were leaving and that another crew would come back in the morning to complete the ME's investigation and retrieve the decedent. He asked, "What am I supposed to do?" My reply was, "Try to stay warm and dry, and they will see you in the morning." His displeasure was palpable. Oh well.

The good doctor and I enjoyed our drive back to the office and said our goodbyes. If memory serves, I filled up the cages that night, completed my paperwork, and gave my report of the night's events to the incoming investigator, along with the pathologists who had come in that morning to perform the autopsies of the day.

I would like to add that the professionalism shown by the pathologists, the autopsy technicians, the office staff, and all the investigators was always impeccable. We, like all other medical professionals, used humor at times to somewhat redirect our thoughts and olfactory senses to something a bit lighter than some of the things with which we had to deal. The decedents were always treated with respect, and the families were assisted in any way we were able. All the cases we took in were required by law to be seen or autopsied at the ME's office. We did not perform cases at the request of the public. I am truly proud and humbled to have worked with such a remarkable group of people. You guys know who you are.

INCIDENT FIFTEEN:
"SUICIDE IS NOT PAINLESS"

Where to start with suicides? I suppose I should describe the many ways one can end one's life. Keep in mind that normally—not always, but normally—the individual's gender and age tend to make a difference in what method is used. Also, one must consider what method is available at the time and place. It can be planned out or it can be spontaneous. It can be self-inflicted, and it can be induced by another, as in "suicide by cop" or stepping off a subway platform at the last second. Firearms are rather popular with adult males, even though I have seen several who hanged themselves. One actually shot himself up intravenously with propofol, a very potent anesthetic. That one was a tad unique.

The reason I wish to approach this topic is because I have dealt with many suicides over both my EMS and death investigation careers, and I want to impress on anyone contemplating suicide that it is, in my opinion, one of the most selfish acts known to man. It may take the person out of their "hell on earth," but it leaves such a lengthy list of problems for those loved ones that are left behind. It adversely affects family and friends not only at the time of the suicide but also for years and years to come. It's a lifelong "gift" that just keeps on giving.

I am going to describe several different suicide scenarios. I may try to inject a bit of humor where I can. Don't be too harsh on me for this; humor is, in fact, the way a lot of us deal with the stark reality of what we have had to witness. This also reminds me of something my youngest son has said many times: "Don't ask dad what he did at work today."

Suicide by Hanging

Like any other EMS call, the alert tones rang out and the dispatcher announced who they needed to respond and what the problem might be. At that point, whatever we were doing had to take second place to the call. One person might be in the day room catching up on the news or weather. Possibly some would be trying their dead level best to catch a nap. Obtaining rest can sometimes feel like trying to catch the next horse on a merry-go-round. If the call came during lunch or dinnertime, everyone assigned to the call would push their plates away and take off for the apparatus bay.

This first case was for a juvenile found in a closet. I can only imagine the horror of a mother walking into her son's bedroom to find what this mother saw. I have no idea what had preceded this event in the young man's mind, only that he had found a permanent solution to what was, I'm sure, a temporary problem.

We marked on the scene and approached the house to see the mother screaming for help. She kept screaming, "MY SON'S NOT BREATHING! MY SON'S NOT BREATHING!"

She was correct. As I approached the boy's bedroom, I could see the room in disarray, the bed unmade, and clothes spread all over the floor—pretty much like many rooms maintained by a teenager. The closet door was on the right side of the room, and it was open about halfway. As I walked around the open door, I found the 14-year-old, blue-eyed, blond boy hanging from the clothes rack with an electrical cord pulling up on his neck. He must have been rather determined to accomplish his task. His legs were bent underneath his slender grey and blueish body. All he had to do to stop, was stand up. He was still dressed in his brown-and-white-striped pajamas. He looked like any other young kid except for the fact he was dead.

87

I did a cursory check for a pulse at his carotid artery and without surprise there was none. Due to experience and the rigidity of his body I determined he had been in this position for some time. Certainly, it was too late for me to remove the snare from his neck and attempt any type of resuscitation. I had the boy's mother and the EMS crew that had arrived leave the room. I notified my dispatcher that we had a DOA (Dead on Arrival), and I requested a police officer to come to the scene.

By this time, we had already stopped using most codes on the radio. Plain language was preferred; however, under this circumstance a code for DOA seemed more appropriate. The young decedent was now a police and medical examiner case.

Since there was nothing I could do for the young man, I turned my attention to the boy's mother. At this point, I cleared the medic unit to go back into service, and I remained behind to obtain information from the mother as well as to attempt to console her. I stayed until the police arrived and gave the responding officer all the information, I had obtained plus anything I could relay about the scene itself. Every time I have had to work with the person left behind, it has taken its toll. It's especially difficult when the loss of a younger child is involved. A parent's brain is just not made to accept the fact that they outlived their child. It's just not the "normal" way of life. However, it happens quite often, and when it does, it takes its toll on everyone involved. I pray to this day that my children outlive me.

After a brief conversation, I simply turned the scene over to the officer. The officer then spoke with the mother a bit and called the medical examiner's office to send an investigator. Having occupied both the position of an EMS captain and a death investigator, I had a good handle on how the flow of events would take place.

I left the scene and headed back to my station. When I arrived, they were getting ready to sit down to eat. Keep in mind this station housed an engine company, a ladder company, a medic unit, a battalion chief, and an EMS captain. There could be as many as twelve men and women sitting down to eat at one time. I walked into the dining area as everyone had just sat down. I filled my plate with whatever Roger, the cook, had prepared and heard him ask, "How many did you kill today?" This, believe it or not, was a running joke. I looked at Roger and said, "Only one so far, but the day is still young."

My responsibility was the entire city, so I usually stayed extremely busy most of the time. That evening I ran two cardiac arrest calls and a shooting; none of whom made it to the hospital alive. I came back into the station later that night, and Lieutenant Roberts, who was the cook, the ladder truck operator, and an all-round good guy, passed by me in the hall while he was on his way to his bunkroom. He turned and said, "You got an update?" My reply was just, "three more." I don't remember laughing too much that evening.

Suicide by Drug Overdose

Same ole same ole; the day had been reasonably busy. In and out of the office, up and down the steps, or occasionally sliding down the long brass pole that led to the main apparatus bay. This time I got called out to one of our outlying areas, and my run time was going to be about fifteen minutes. I advised the dispatcher that I was on the way. As I started down the streets with my lights flashing and my siren blaring, I picked up my microphone and advised the medic unit and engine company, also responding to the call, that I would be about ten minutes behind them.

After they arrived on the scene, they found a distraught man about sixty-five years old, and he led them to where he had found his wife. She was supine on the bed with a nice clean dress on. If she had not been dead as three o'clock, she could have been mistaken for just taking a nap. Then there was the stream of vomit stringing from her mouth onto the pillow and bed.

When I arrived, the medic, another David P., advised me of his findings and that the woman had apparently been deceased for at least a couple of hours. Once again in this type of situation, there had been no attempt at resuscitation, nor should there be. I wrote down on my notepad the information given by the medic and released the unit to go back into service along with the engine company.

I called dispatch and asked for an ETA for the responding officer. Keep in mind, the police don't consider a DOA to need a rapid response. Sometimes, depending on call levels, the officer my take thirty minutes or so.

Here again I am with a family member who has been cheated out of whatever kind of relationship they had with the person. Whether their story was good, bad, or indifferent, the end was written by the woman on the bed. I found an empty bottle of an opioid that had been recently prescribed. It had been filled with sixty little white tablets, and they were all gone. I could assume that she had taken the pills, but it was ultimately the medical examiner's decision to declare. I jotted down my notes and went in to speak with the husband who was openly sobbing. The realization that his wife had died finally hit him. I put my hand on his shoulder and tried to console him to no avail.

I have said "I'm so very sorry for your loss" a thousand times. I try to make it come out with feeling, and I want the one left behind to realize my empathy. But to be honest, sometimes it's very difficult. Sometimes I think it comes out sounding rather shallow and uncaring. I think maybe after saying it so many times, my heart is just not always in it. One tends to get callous over time. The effect of doing this repeatedly is accumulative. As I write these words, I feel sort of numb with a hint of melancholy.

Suicide by Gun

Ahh yes, one of my favorites…NOT. When someone takes their own life, you must figure they are at a low, low spot in their mind. I've heard it described as if they were in a dark room with no windows and no doors. They couldn't see their own hand in front of their face, and it became painfully obvious that they would never be able to find a way out—except for possibly the pistol or rifle or shotgun sitting beside them. The sadness and pain were palpable. I've heard this from several people who had attempted and failed. Some of them do it again, and some ultimately find a safe way out.

The person in this story did not find that path out. At one point, I was a preceptor with a local health science college. I would take green paramedic students out on calls and let them do as much as possible with me looking over their shoulders. We responded to a call for a possible suicide, and we talked a little bit on the way, discussing the different ways to kill oneself. If one has never been around people in the medical field, that kind of conversation might sound kind of strange. In this situation, it was very normal and educational for the students.

We arrived on the scene, and even though it was a possible suicide, there was no need to wait for police. The caller had told dispatch that the individual was sitting in a chair, not moving, and appeared deceased.

When approaching any type of call that may involve violence, one should be very cautious. One of the students started to knock on the door, and I told him to stand to the side of the door when knocking. It doesn't really matter what kind of call one is on; caution should be observed regardless.

A woman came to the door and just said, "He's in there." She had pointed to a bedroom door. Picture this: on this call we have an EMT driver, two paramedic students, and me. The student who was taking the lead on this call entered the room first. I was close behind. We saw a very slender elderly man sitting up in his chair, which was positioned against a wall. There was a twelve-gauge, single-shot shotgun between his legs and leaning upon his shoulder. On observation, he appeared to not be breathing, and he was not moving. One of the students said, "Let's get him to the floor," and was planning to start CPR and run a "code blue" on the man. I put my hand out and stopped the student from touching the man. I then said check his pulse, which he did and found none. The wife was still in the other room, and I told the student to look at the back of the man's head. He checked and gasped. The back of his head was pretty much splattered all over the wall.

The man had placed the shotgun in his mouth and blew the back of his head off. The lesson here was that tunnel vision is not a good thing. One should always make a basic assessment of the situation and the patient before moving a body, which very well could compromise a possible crime scene. In this situation, we notified our dispatcher that we needed an officer to respond to our location for a DOA.

Suicide by Taking a Leap

I have seen several jumpers over the years, and most of them accomplish their task and end up in the morgue. I have seen a few who failed—either they needed a higher object to jump from or something harder to hit.

One of my co-workers was on a call for a lady threatening suicide as she stood on the edge of a pretty high bridge. The police were trying to talk her down when she jumped and landed with a large, loud splash. She hit flat on the water. She then stood up in about two feet of water, and said, "SHIT!!!" She walked out of the water and ended up in a psychiatric ward.

When they end up with a couple of broken legs or no injuries at all, it's always sad for them and they usually say something like, "Damnit, I can't even do that right." What can you say? "Better luck next time?" Probably not appropriate, but it would be tempting.

On the other hand, if people think this method out a little more. most do not survive the pull of gravity. We have had them jump from bridges, high-rise buildings, parking garages, and about anything else they can find that will offer the anticipated sudden stop with the appropriate ending. Sad, but true.

Suicide by "Seppuku" AKA "Hara-kiri"

This is one of the reasons this book would have to receive at the very least an "R" rating if it were a movie—not a story for the grandkids.

Here we go again; we were dispatched to assist police with a possible suicide. In this case, the police had been called prior to fire-EMS, and they had already arrived. Upon our arrival, the officer asked for only one paramedic to enter the apartment to pronounce the person dead. I spoke with the officer before going in, and he said police had been called for a "well-being check" and had to force their way into the apartment. He said what they found was the most bizarre thing he had ever seen. Well, when a seasoned sergeant who is near retirement makes that kind of statement, it makes the hair on the back of your neck stand erect. I entered and, once again, was very careful where I walked, but I gazed at the room in amazement for a moment. The officer stood beside me, and we both tried to wrap our brains around what we were seeing. Sometimes things are so crazy—or as the officer put it, bizarre— that it's difficult for the brain to readily process the images it sees.

In this scene, there were cut marks all over the walls. It reminded me of a Freddy Krueger movie. However, this was not Elm Street, and this definitely was no movie. All the furniture was slashed with the stuffing all over the floor. There were paintings and pictures on the wall, either slashed or the glass broken. There was a large kitchen knife covered in blood in the middle of the kitchen floor. My eyes then turned to the hallway going back toward two separate bedrooms. There were strange bloody tracks that looked at first like a body had been dragged down the hall, but the tracks were so even and defined. Blood splatter was all over the floor but only so far up the walls. That became a quick pattern that the officer had noticed, as did I. He directed me to the first bedroom. As I looked inside the doorway, I could see where the mattress had been slashed just like the chairs and sofa. Once again blood was everywhere. It was difficult to avoid stepping in the blood on the floor. With this amount of blood, I was almost expecting to see several people bludgeoned to death. But we entered the last bedroom, and the subject who had apparently caused all the damage to the apartment had found his final resting place for the day. Once again, all the furniture and walls were cut and slashed. Blood was all over the floor and the bed as well as the walls. The reason the blood and the damage only went so high on the walls was that the man was wheelchair-bound. He was former military and had been injured in Vietnam.

His pale body was still sitting in the wheelchair, and the chair was leaning over onto the side of the bed. All the tracks in the hallway were made when he had gone to get and bring back another butcher knife. The poor haunted soul turned that knife on himself and eviscerated himself from sea to shiny sea. His intestines laid out on his lap. You could also see where he had cut his legs completely to the bone just above the knees. He had also slashed both wrists to the bone. This was an easy one to pronounce dead. May God have mercy on his soul.

INCIDENT SIXTEEN:
"A GOOD DAY? NO, A GREAT DAY!"

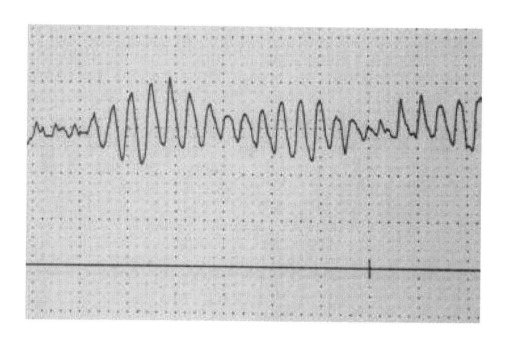

Let's go back in time just a little. This next incident was early in my career with the city. I was a paramedic working on an ambulance with a partner. Rick and I had been through a lot together. We had studied for our exams for shock trauma, cardiac tech, and paramedic together. He was a friend long before we started working at the same place. I dare say we both were extremely comfortable with one another's capabilities, and we were almost at the point of finishing each other's sentences. This was back in the days of the city's third service EMS system, long before we merged with the fire department. When we responded to a call, we were pretty much it unless we could get another medic unit to assist from across town. Sometimes, we even responded alone in an ambulance. That was known as the dreaded code-57.

It was about eight a.m. on a Monday, and I arrived as usual about a half-hour before shift change. Per normal, we chatted for a short period of time, and Rick and I received a turnover from the medics on their way out the door. Rick and I sat down, each with a nice hot cup of coffee when, yep, a call goes out and the irritating tones ring just before the dispatcher makes her announcement. The call was for a possible "code blue." The address given was only about three minutes away.

As the dispatcher was repeating her announcement with the same information, we had already started en route to the scene.

When responding to someone complaining of a hurt arm or a broken finger or any other common or mundane call, EMS crews normally go with haste but not necessarily with great speed. When someone is possibly in cardiac arrest, the pace generally picks up a bit.

As I stated, our station was fairly near this call, and that, quite frankly, generally gives the patient a better shot at survival. As we careened through rush hour traffic, with lights flashing and siren blaring, to our amazement cars and trucks that could have very easily delayed our response quickly moved over and out of our way.

Our response time was just over three minutes. We arrived on scene, and I climbed out of the passenger's side and Rick from the driver's side of the vehicle, now sitting silently in the middle of a small business parking lot. The bright flashing red-and-white lights were still announcing to the passersby of someone's urgent need for assistance. We grabbed the equipment possibly needed for this type of call. I walked in with the Lifepak 5, which was a cardiac monitor/defibrillator used in the early- to mid-80s, and a jump kit containing IV supplies, a blood pressure cuff, a stethoscope, and a multitude of other assorted items. Rick had in hand the "airway kit" along with an oxygen tank and the drug box.

As stated earlier, we didn't have an extra nearby crew or the fire department responding with us on medical calls. We could request the fire department, but everyone was hesitant to call them because most of the firefighters did not want to get involved in medical "stuff." That's a very long chapter by itself, so I will let that one slide for now.

As we approached the front of the small business, a man came out and yelled for us to hurry! When one is carrying half of the equipment from the guts of a medic unit, one can only hurry so much—just sayin'.

We entered the lobby to find a man doing CPR on a poor soul laying supine on the floor. The patient was extremely cyanotic, meaning he was blue to the point of resembling a large Smurf. The gentleman that was performing CPR was doing a pretty good job, so as my partner and I made ready for what we were about to do to this lifeless body, I encouraged the Good Samaritan to continue. I also recommended he push a little deeper and a bit faster, and he did quite well.

To this day, I believe the Good Samaritan, who was the patient's co-worker, gave his friend the best chance for a positive outcome. My partner keyed his radio's mic and requested assistance for a "code blue."

I tore open the patient's shirt, exposing his chest, so that I might try to discover exactly what was happening to the man's heart. I turned on the monitor and pulled the paddles from their holder on the defibrillator. I then took the little tube of defib gel and pushed out a small amount on the metal plate that covered one of the paddles. Then I rubbed the paddles together to cover both plates with gel and placed them in the appropriate locations on the patient's chest. By this time, my partner had begun hyperventilating the patient in anticipation of an endotracheal intubation. This would give us the ultimate access to the patient's airway so that we could not only breathe for the gentleman but protect the airway from further encroachments.

By pressing the paddles on the subject's chest, I could obtain a reading of the electrical activity of the man's heart. I gazed at the monitor as I told everyone to take their hands off the patient for a moment. Across the front of the monitor came a tracing that all medics easily recognize called "coarse ventricular fibrillation (V-fib)." The patient needed to be shocked. I had Rick and the co-worker continue CPR as I set the dial for the correct amount of current, measured in joules, that I needed to transverse the patient's heart. I then depressed the black button to charge the paddles. A shrill, audible alert made sure all realized the paddles were being charged.

I exclaimed "Clear, Clear, Clear" as I made sure both the man still doing CPR and my partner's hands and knees were not in contact with the patient. Then I looked back at the monitor, confirming the dysrhythmia. I pressed the paddles on the patient's chest and simultaneously depressed the two red buttons, one on each paddle, as the patient's body suddenly responded with a jerk. Rick quickly checked the patient's carotid pulse and confirmed it was still absent, with the comment, "No pulse." Glancing at the monitor, I still saw V-fib, and once again one could hear the shrill alert, "Clear, Clear, Clear," and SHOCK. The patient's body again jerked as his hands slightly came away from the floor and then back down at rest.

This time, when I glanced at the monitor, I noticed a rhythm began to bounce across the little screen. I hit the button to turn on the recording, and a strip of his electrical activity was generated on a special thermal paper. I had the man's friend discontinue CPR. My partner was still maintaining the man's airway, and he checked the patient's carotid pulse and still there was none. This happens quite often, and then the patient deteriorates into their previous state and the outcome is extremely negative.

Rick placed a laryngoscope, which is a metal blade with a light at the end, down the patient's throat so he could see the patient's open vocal cords. This procedure is done to maintain total control over a patient's airway and prepare for an endotracheal tube insertion. As Rick approached the cords, he got a bit of a surprise—the man began to gag. I noted another rhythm change on the EKG, which was now showing a viable rhythm. Another check and I stated rather succinctly, "We have a pulse." The second medic unit then arrived, which gave us two more sets of skilled hands to accomplish the tasks required.

The patient's pulse got stronger, and the monitor's screen showed a rhythm requiring drug therapy. Once again, a strip was run off and evaluated. An IV was initiated with a bag of D5W (5% dextrose in sterile water), which would facilitate the delivery of much needed medication.

The patient was still unconscious and his body flaccid; however, his skin color had changed from a dark blue to a lighter shade of pale. Very promising indeed.

Rick had dropped in a nasal airway and by utilizing the bag-valve mask, kept the man well ventilated.

I picked up the ole trusty Advanced Portable Coronary Observation Radio (APCOR) and contacted the hospital. This was before the field medics were able to administer certain medications prior to advising the hospital and obtaining direction. We administered the appropriate medications and began transporting the patient to the hospital emergency department.

En route to the hospital, the patient's level of consciousness increased; he became combative for a short period and then calmed down. To my surprise, he began to try to speak, and before we made it to the hospital, he looked at me and asked what had happened and where he was. I simply lied and said, "You just passed out and we are on our way to the hospital to get you checked out." I was afraid if I told him the truth, I'd scare him to death.

We turned him over to the ED with stable vital signs, and he was still alert and oriented. I overheard him ask the doctor what had happened, and the doc said, "Those people just saved your life." I walked away feeling like that day was indeed a great day.

The patient went into cardiac arrest two more times during his stay in the cardiac care unit. He was resuscitated both times and ultimately had a cardiac catheterization performed and stints inserted to keep his arteries open. He was released to go home not long after that.

I went back to check on him a couple of times at his business, and he was doing extremely well.

About ten years had passed and I was driving around town in my emergency vehicle, making my daily rounds at work, and I received a call from the ED Med-Com. The caller said he had a lady who wanted to speak to me. I listened and this lady said," I don't know if you remember me or my husband or not, but you and your friends saved his life at his place of business." She gave me his name, and I told her that I did remember. She said that she had some bad news. He had just died in the ED with a massive heart attack, and that she wanted to thank us for giving her ten additional years with her husband. I was virtually speechless. I told her how sorry I was for her loss and God bless. I also told her I would relay her words to my co-workers and how much her words were appreciated.

We rarely ever followed up on patients; we had so many of them. This lady took the time and trouble just to say thank you. That phone call was one of the most important and memorable calls I have ever had.

INCIDENT SEVENTEEN:
"DRIVE IN"

Sarah and I were sitting in the day room of Station 4 not long after returning from a failed "Code Blue"—probably talking about what we could have done differently or maybe just chatting about me not wanting to watch her soap opera.

We met on the first day of my professional career as a paramedic. She was the volunteer crews first lieutenant and had been running calls for many years. She was about ten years my senior, not very tall, and slightly plump—plus one of the nicest individuals I had ever met. We really did click right off the bat. She definitely knew her stuff and quickly gained my respect not only as a person but as an accomplished EMT as well. She respected my training even though she had much more experience than I.

Sarah and I were watching TV and having a cup of coffee when we both heard a horn blowing outside the station. We went to the door and heard a woman sitting in her car screaming, "My baby's not breathing, HELP, HELP!" We approached the car to find an infant in a car seat truly not breathing. The child had apparently had a previous problem of some sort because she had a stoma cut into her neck. Her breathing was totally dependent on the stoma. Sometimes a stoma can get clogged and that can create a problem with breathing, but at that time, it really didn't matter much what had caused it. We just needed to solve the current pressing problem. I tilted the infant's head back to expose the stoma, and as I did, I asked her mother if this had happened before. The mother said it had not. I asked Sarah to get an obstetrical (OB) kit and a suction unit from the ambulance as I stayed with the infant.

She returned with the equipment as well as an intubation kit and an oxygen tank. I opened the OB kit and pulled out a bulb syringe. I tried to suction the stoma, which appeared to be clogged, but the tip in the bulb syringe was too large. I just couldn't get a good enough seal to make it work. We didn't have the equipment for a stoma that small. At that time in the existence of the system, our equipment catered toward adults and children but not for neonates or very small infants.

The baby girl by this time was totally flaccid and rapidly turning blue. I took one of the suction tubes and whittled it down with a knife until I could introduce it into the stoma. I carefully suctioned the stoma and her larynx until it was clear and then took the O2 line, connected it to a fourteen-gauge angiocath and administered oxygen. Within moments, she started to breathe on her own, and she quickly lost the prevalent blueish tint. We loaded the little lady into our medic unit and advised dispatch we were en route to the ED with a walk-in patient. Mom followed in her car.

Our small patient did extremely well, and I notified the hospital that we did not have the proper equipment for such a small patient. Not too long after, we updated our "stuff" to accommodate the younger population.

I assumed the little tike did OK and really didn't give it another thought until a year later when I was sitting in the same station and that same mother knocked on the door. She said that she had someone in her car she wanted to show me. I walked out, and mom was smiling from ear to ear. She simply said, "I just wanted to come by and say thank you and to show you what you did."

I told her how much I appreciated her coming by that day, and she returned to that station and to every station I worked, at least once every two or three years. When the child was old enough to understand what her mother was talking about, her mother would say, "This is the man who saved your life." Once again, I would be speechless.

The last time I saw the mother and her daughter, the daughter was about fifteen years old. The mother, just like so many times before, proudly stated, "This man saved your life."

Only a few times in one's career does one get such a return from their investment. I'll never forget that tiny girl in the car seat or her mother.

INCIDENT EIGHTEEN:
"MURDER/SUICIDE"

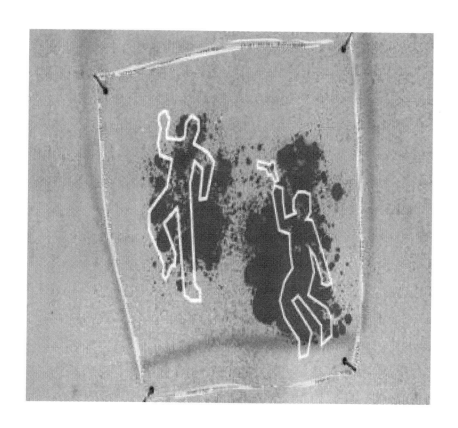

Working with the medical examiner's office is a bit different from working for fire-EMS. No loud tones, no announcements over the loudspeakers—for that matter, no loudspeakers. As I previously stated, I worked midnights at the ME's office, and unless I had a phone call from a police officer or a medical institution, requesting my presence, my work would be done on a computer and a phone.

In our office, we would regularly have twenty to thirty case files on our desk on any normal day or night. This night had gone fairly calmly, and the sun was peeking through the window. I was hoping for a quick turnover and looking forward to laying my head on my pillow. Then the phone rang and the officer on the other end of the phone said he had two victims. He stated that some idiot had chased his girlfriend from her apartment to a nearby street corner and completed their argument in a definitive way. I packed up my jump kit and my camera equipment, walked to the vehicle bay, and went on my merry way.

Note again the difference between EMS and ME: no hurry, no siren, no weaving in and out of cars and trucks. This time, I followed the rules and regulations of the road.

It really did make this job a lot easier. The police, I knew, would be on the scene and it would be completely secured. I wouldn't have to be concerned about weapons being drawn and ready to use. For that matter, all I had to be concerned about was just doing my scene investigation and getting the decedents back to the office.

I arrived to find two subjects down on a street corner, in plain view of every car that was driving by. The "rubbernecking" drivers were going crazy. Why we didn't already have two or three car crashes I'll never know. The police had obtained a large amount of black plastic, and they made a barrier so that the public would not be able to see the decedents, me, or any of the officers working the scene. I'll have to admit that made the scene much more compatible for what we were about to do.

The first thing the police would do on a case such as this would be to make sure the scene was secure from anyone else with a gun. Before they could make an assumption of murder/suicide, they would need to eyeball the scene and get information from any available witnesses. I believe in this situation witnesses were easy to find, and they were readily able to conclude that these two were the only subjects involved.

After the police performed their preliminary investigation, they would normally give the ME's office a call and request our company on the scene. This is what had just occurred.

Unless given permission over the phone, the police would not move the body until the ME investigator had arrived and completed their own on-scene investigation. That investigation involved first photographing the general scene around the decedents. If a street sign or a building was nearby, that would be incorporated into the photos to show the location. Closer photos then would be taken but still not really close up. While using still photography, I tried to make it appear as if one was walking up to the crime scene.

The police had not located any spent casings from the weapon of choice, a 9 mm semi-automatic pistol, so I assisted in the search. Even though two shots had been fired from the pistol, we found only one casing on the ground. The other one was lodged in the pistol and had not ejected. I placed an evidence ruler marked with the case number and my initials beside any object to be photographed. I shot pictures of the casing on the ground from a distance, showing location, and then close up. I took photos of the pistol with the casing lodged in the ejection port. I once again placed the ruler next to the pistol for case identification as well as for the investigator working the case.

The photograph below is an example of a scene photo, and I should add it has nothing to do with this or any other case. After the photos were finished of the periphery, additional photos were taken of the decedents. Again, first I took photos at a distance and then closer. I took photos of any obvious identifying tattoos along with close-ups of all obvious wounds.

The decedent's hands were photographed and then placed inside paper bags to preserve any evidence that may be later found on them or under the fingernails. Occasionally, we would swab the hands for gunshot residue, but normally we simply bagged the hands. The bags were then secured at the wrist with evidence tape and the tape initialed by the investigator. (Page 104)

5.56 rifle casing along with evidence marker

Example of how to use an evidence bag to protect any evidence on a body's hands
(with initialed tape and evidence marker)

After the decedent's hands had been bagged, the investigator along with the police would roll the decedent onto their other side, and the photos would continue until anything and everything that could be construed as possible evidence was in the camera's memory card. The police evidence technician would also photograph the decedents after they had been rolled over.

In this incident, it appeared that the male had shot the female and then turned the weapon on himself. Thus, it was a presumed murder/suicide case, although not official until the OCME's pathologist said so.

It was then time to place identification tags on the decedent's large toes—a.k.a. toe tags—and place both bodies inside body bags. Anything attached to the body went with the investigator, and anything not actually attached would be documented and the police would take as evidence.

After the large, usually black, heavy-duty plastic bag was zipped up, another tag was filled out and placed through the zipper tabs with the same information that was on the toe tag. Everything would have been initialed by the ME's investigator on the scene.

Now it would be time for moving the decedent's bodies. In this instance, we had a good deal of cover from the plastic walls that the police had erected. I backed the van up close to the "wall," and the officers assisted in moving the bodies from their present resting places to the next, which would be a ride to the morgue.

After arriving at the morgue, the bodies would be transferred from the van to the intake cooler and placed in a locked cage. This would allow for a solid "chain of evidence."

Now, the paperwork would begin. Remember, our job was to determine the cause and manner of death, and the police had to try to figure out who and why. The "who" would come, in part, from the autopsies. The why would take some more investigation by the police.

After making ready the basic report and completing the appropriate labels for the day's autopsies, my work was almost complete. The graveyard shift was nearly over.

Shortly after everyone showed up for the day's work, we had a morning meeting consisting of the oncoming investigators, the pathologists, and the staff. Generally, those meetings were very succinct and to the point.

Home was the next stop, and an attempt to get some sleep before the next night shift. Have any of you ever tried to sleep in the daytime?

INCIDENT NINETEEN:
"CLOSE CALL"

Helicopters are giant, magnificently constructed flying machines. First, a brief history lesson from Wikipedia: "On September 14, 1939, the VS-300, the world's first practical helicopter, took flight at Stratford, Connecticut. Designed by Igor Sikorsky and built by the Vought-Sikorsky Aircraft Division of the United Aircraft Corporation, the helicopter was the first to incorporate a single main rotor and tail rotor design." With that said, they are really a lot of fun to fly in.

The first "bird" I flew in was a Bell 206 Jet Ranger (Page 110). It was a small aircraft, compared to some others, but very agile. When we carried a patient on board, we had to remove the co-pilots seat to make room. The flight medic's access was limited to the patient's waist and above. This configuration obviously made working on the patient a bit difficult. The next one purchased by the hospital was a Bell 222A. What a fine ship she was. This ship allowed two medical attendants, so at that point flight nurses were introduced into the program. We were also able to handle two patients at a time when the need arose.

Do any of you remember the TV show *Airwolf*? That flying machine was also a Bell 222. By the way, they do not fly upside down like on TV. I'm not sure if I can get away with showing this photo of Airwolf I found online, but here it is: Airwolf 222 and, below, a photo I took of our Bell 222A. (Page 111.)

On page 112, you will find a photo of the last bird I worked out of: a Bell 412SP; a fine piece of work and packed with the latest medical equipment.

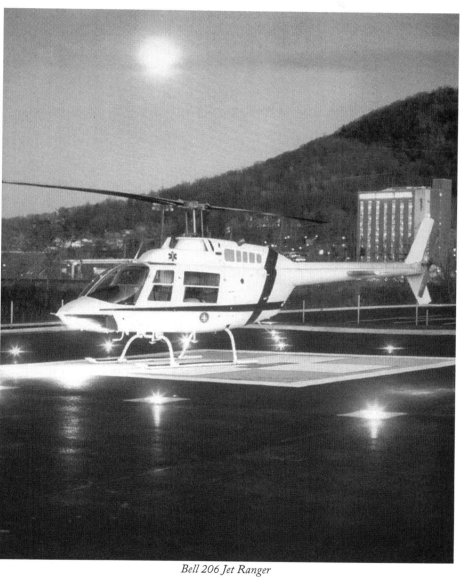

Bell 206 Jet Ranger

Bell 222A (the helicopter from Airwolf, top, and our ship)

Some of the finest and most professional people I have ever known.

Bell 412SP

Now, to get back to the story. We were flying, scud running as it were (flying below the low-lying clouds and following a highway). We probably should have filed an Instrument Flight Rules (IFR) flight plan, risen above the clouds, flown back to the airport, and then to the helipad, but for some reason we did not. The 222 cruised along at about 120 knots, which is about 140 m.p.h. We were headed back from a flight without a patient on board, and all was calm and normal. I was in one of the back seats on this flight, the pilot and nurse in the front. It was going to be a long flight, so I had almost dozed off due to the thump, thump, thump vibrations of the bird. All of a sudden the pilot yelled, "Look Left! Look Left!" As I started to look out the left-side window, the 222 sharply banked to the right and I saw the belly of a twin-engine airplane zip by. Apparently, the twin was scud running at the same altitude but in the opposite direction at about 200 m.p.h. Thank God, both pilots acted swiftly and appropriately, both banking right to avoid a collision. Pucker factor of 10.

The next close encounter that really got my attention happened in the larger and third helicopter we flew in at the trauma center. This was a Bell 412SP. The 412 could carry four patients and four medical attendants, as well as two folks upfront keeping the machine up in the air and bringing us down safely.

Make no mistake, most of the pilots at this service were excellent and made very few, if any, mistakes. We easily trusted them with our lives. They were the best of the best. Several had flown in Vietnam, and their skill level was at the top of the game. Occasionally, a pilot would sign on and would not have the experience of most of the others. This was one such pilot and here is the story.

Lynne K., a very accomplished and seasoned flight nurse; the pilot, who we'll call Jack; and I had been sitting around late one evening and had just finished dinner when the phone rang, and it was a request for a site response from an EMS agency for a farmer who had been hurt by a machine rolling over. He had been pinned underneath the machine for an hour or so. The fire department and the EMS crew had removed him from his unfortunate predicament and were treating his injuries in the ambulance. His condition was severe enough that they appropriately believed their patient would greatly benefit from a rapid transport to the trauma center rather than the hour-long ambulance run from that outlying area.

The drill was much the same every time we received a flight request. The pilot would immediately check the weather situation as the medical crew obtained as much information as possible from the dispatcher.

On this flight, Jack climbed in the right front seat as usual, and Lynne took a seat in the back. I put on my helmet, picked up the handle that was connected to the box containing the auxiliary batteries, rolled it to the front of the aircraft, and plugged it into the auxiliary power unit (APU) port on the nose of the red, white, and blue beast. I then connected my communication line into the outside receptacle. With the helmet on and the com-line plugged in, I would be able to talk with the pilot.

Standing outside of one of these huge machines as the twin jet engines roar to life was an exhilarating feeling. As the turbines turned and the main rotor started to rotate, I could hear even with the helmet on, the blades cutting through the air with that familiar repetitive thumping sound and eventually one's chest would start to vibrate. Then the pilot said on the headset, as well as with a thumbs up, to disconnect the APU. I rolled it to the side of the helipad and climbed into the co-pilot's left side front seat.

The machine began to vibrate a bit more and as the heavy aircraft started to lift from the concrete pad, the pilot advised the trauma center dispatcher we were en route, and then he alerted the local airport controller we were on a "lifeguard" mission and our anticipated destination. As I mentioned earlier, "Lifeguard" is the designation air ambulances use to identify when they are on a mission with a patient or on the way to a patient in need.

The sun had passed below the mountains, and the lights from the cars and trucks tracing the roads were apparent as well as the twinkle from all the other lights on the ground below. The flight to the scene was uneventful. As we approached, we could see the landing zone (LZ) the fire trucks had outlined in a field. Generally, they would form a triangle with their headlights, and the LZ would be the center of the triangle. We were slowing down and reducing altitude and again everything so far was per usual when I noticed a large tree to left and below, so I advised Jack, over the intercom, that we had a tree to the left and it was directly below us.

Ninety-nine percent of the time when any of the flight crew said something to the pilot during a descent it was immediately acknowledged and acted upon if required. This was not at all unusual. Part of the job of the flight medic and the flight nurse was to help the pilot look out for obstacles, whether flying along, taking off, or landing.

I noted on the intercom once again that there was a tree, and by this time, I even identified it as an oak tree. Once again, Jack did not acknowledge. Keep in mind we were sitting side by side and within arm's reach. I tapped him on the shoulder and said, "Jack we have a tree and need to bump up." He just looked at me and continued the descent. By this time Lynne was joining in the conversation as our voices became alarmed. The skids of the helicopter were beginning to touch the upper limbs of the tree, and we both yelled at Jack, and I hit him on the shoulder. He then pulled slightly up on the collective as he pressed forward on the cyclic. This allowed the bird to climb a bit and then we drifted forward and then down again. In unison, Lynne and I yelled, "JACK, THE TAIL ROTOR, THE TAIL ROTOR!" He bumped up slightly again, and we went just beyond the tree and landed safely in the field.

Honestly, I had been flying for about six years and had flown with a lot of different pilots, but this one scared the hell out of me. I swear, Lynne and I climbed out of the bird with the rotors still whipping around. We met in the front of the bird and literally hugged each other.

We then turned to meet the first responders on the ground. One older firefighter walked up to me and said, "Hell, I thought y'all was goners." I replied, "So did I, so did I." We attended to our patient's needs and placed him in the helicopter as we both this time crawled into the back with the patient. We did our thing, starting IV lines and hooking up a couple of machines to keep tabs on his heart, his blood pressure, and O2 saturation. We took the information we had been given by the ground crew, compiled a bit more on our flight back, and relayed that report to the trauma center. We landed at the hospital without incident and turned our patient over to the trauma team waiting in the ED.

I recall going back to our quarters and Lynne and I discussing what we should do. For the safety of all involved, we decided to file a formal complaint on Jack and handed it in to the powers-that-be.

We both hated that we had to file that report because we both really liked him a lot. He was really a great guy, just not as great in the right-hand seat at night. If memory serves, he was reprimanded and had to go through some retraining and eventually was transferred to another location.

The other close calls were much less dramatic, and one even involved a couple of military jets out playing around.

Flying with that air medical service was one of my finest jobs, and the people I worked with, to this day, remain good friends. The respect I had and still have for those pilots, nurses, and paramedics is enormous.

INCIDENT TWENTY:
"TOO CLOSE TO HOME"

As I previously stated, I started my first responder career as a volunteer in a rural county. It was an exceptionally large county, so sometimes the response times were extremely long, but occasionally, it would strike close to home. For this incident, I had just returned home from a shift in the city and was about to settle down for breakfast before I headed off to bed.

This was me, back in the day. I had a dark brown mustache and dark hair.
Hell, I had hair!!!

I wonder how many of you remember the old Plectron receivers (see photo)? The tones it broadcast were different for the varied number of rescue squads that served the entire county. Dispatchers back then were not only EMS and fire dispatchers but also served the Sheriff's department.

Plectron receiver

The tones would ring out, and if you didn't recognize the tones you would have to wait until the broadcast was almost finished to hear if they were calling your crew out. This time the alert was for my little rural rescue squad. It was for a possible heart attack. The sad part was the address was not far from my house, and I knew the sweet dear lady who lived there. She had lost her husband of fifty-five years not long before that, and she lived by herself. Her son lived nearby and had been with her when she fell ill. I ran out the door and with my portable radio advised that I was on my way—10-76 back then as we still were using 10-codes.

I arrived within a couple of minutes on scene and began to assess my patient/friend. No matter how many patients one has worked on, it is always a bit different when it's someone you know and really care about.

She was about eighty-six years old and had lived the life of a farmer's wife. She had three grown children and several grandchildren. When I walked into the room, she was sitting bolt upright with obvious respiratory distress. I asked her what was bothering her the most, and she said in short broken sentences that it was hard for her to breathe. I checked her pulse, and it was thready, but I could feel missed beats and the rate was a bit rapid. I checked her blood pressure, and she was hypertensive. I noticed that both of her lower legs were rather swollen and that her respirations were increasingly labored. I put a non-rebreather mask on her with high-flow O2 and started an IV with D5W, knowing she would require drug therapy as soon as the ambulance arrived.

It was going to be at least another ten to fifteen minutes before more help would make it there, so I sat with my old friend and tried to make her as comfortable as possible. The worry in the room was palpable, and small talk was about all we could produce.

When the ambulance arrived, we put our patient on the stretcher and rolled her out of her house, possibly for the last time. We had about a thirty-five- to forty-minute ride to the hospital ahead of us. I must admit, I said a few prayers during that ride. I put the little pads on her chest and turned on the EKG to find no major surprise. Her heart was in atrial fibrillation, a rhythm that often accompanies congestive heart failure (CHF). We started running hard and fast toward the hospital, and I popped open the drug box and pulled out a vial of Lasix and an ampoule of morphine. The Lasix was for the excessive fluid that had built up in her lungs, and the morphine was to help calm her as well as disperse some of the fluid in a slightly different way.

I'll have to admit I was one tired and worried paramedic. The morphine seemed to ease her just a bit, but the concern was written all over her face. I had treated her for CHF a couple of times over the past few years, but this time was different, and she fully well knew it. She looked at me as we were about halfway to the hospital and said, "I'm not going to make it this time." Just as simple as that.

I've learned over the thirty years of working the streets that when someone tells you that they are not going to make it, you need to take heed because there seems to be this internal clock that they feel ticking its last few ticks.

I gave her a bit more Lasix and morphine before we arrived at the hospital. She and I were always able to make each other smile. I loved that sweet ole lady. This time no smiles, she just said, "Thank you for all you did for Herman and me over the years." Then she added, "Goodbye." I think we both knew that that goodbye was probably going to be the last.

We arrived at the hospital, pulled the stretcher from the back of the unit, and wheeled her inside to meet the medical teams. I gave my turnover to the nurses and doctors who had been waiting for us. I remember bending over and giving her a little kiss on the forehead before I left the emergency room. She passed away later that day. I still miss her and think of her often.

INCIDENT TWENTY-ONE:
"COINCIDENCE OR FATE"

Arson is a terrible thing. And when someone decides it's fun and commits that dangerous and felonious act multiple times, well, the only thing one can do is try their best to catch the arsonist before they kill someone.

We, the fire-EMS Department, had been called out for a dumpster fire, and it only takes one engine company to quickly extinguish the nuisance fire and then return to their station. But keep in mind that during that dumpster fire the engine company couldn't respond to potential real emergencies, such as a structure fire with someone trapped or an EMS call where the EMTs and paramedics on the engine company could have arrived and saved a life. The dumpster fire would then become a possible contributing factor to an unnecessary death. It would no longer be considered just a nuisance.

We had received calls for several such fires and then a structure fire in the same vicinity. The structure fire takes more time and manpower to put out and then return to the station. It was an abandoned boarded-up house. No electrical service was found and no reason for an accidental fire. Arson was highly suspected.

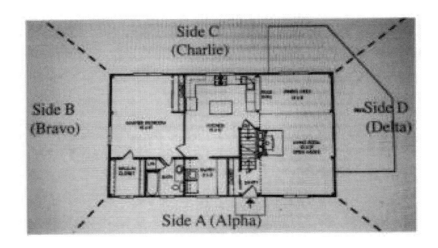

The above diagram shows the typical layout of a single-story structure fire. Side A (Alpha) is the address, entry, or street side.

The following shift (B-Shift) had to return to the same area of the city the next night for another structure fire. Both houses were abandoned, and the risk at that point was to the firefighters rather than an occupant.

C-Shift received another call for a structure fire in the same general area. Needless to say, the number of fires and their similar locations alerted the fire marshal as well as the police.

The following night, A-Shift was back on duty, and the battalion chiefs along with the police and I drove through that general vicinity up until about three a.m. The chiefs returned, as did I, to our respective stations while the police continued to patrol through the night. This continued for several nights, and nothing appeared out of the ordinary. For some reason, the arsonist seemed to be attached to that one section of the city. With all the visible patrols, I suppose the arsonist laid low and apparently didn't want to get caught.

A few nights had passed, and all had been quiet as far as fires went. Then another fire call went out not too far from those prior locations. This time it was not abandoned, and the price of poker went way up. We arrived on scene to a two-story wood frame structure with flames and smoke showing from sides A and B. The first company to arrive entered with a line from their engine. This meant the water supply was limited to the amount carried in their tank, which was approximately five-hundred gallons. That will only last so long.

As other engine companies and a ladder company arrived, a water supply was established, and the battalion chief took command of the fire ground operations. I was assigned to EMS division, and within minutes of arriving, I was advised that a subject was found in the house and was being passed through a first-floor window. The medic unit personnel and I went to the location the interior group had identified as a window on side 1-Bravo. As I approached the window, the firefighters were passing the lifeless body out to me. The body was covered in soot and residue from the smoke and fire. It turned out to be an elderly lady. I did not expect for her be alive. Most of the time, under similar circumstances, she would have been DOA. Or sometimes we would call them DRT (dead right there). Just to verify that she was dead, I checked for a carotid pulse, and low and behold, she had a very weak pulse. She was not breathing, but with a pulse present, it was time for me to go to work.

I alerted the two paramedics from the standby unit, and they joined the action. We moved the patient away from the smoke and heat of the fire and started to attempt to resuscitate her. I remember bagging her (ventilating with a bag-valve mask) for a short time and then intubating. One of the other medics put on the EKG pads and confirmed that we did, in fact, have cardiac activity. It was initially very bradycardic (slow), but after I intubated and started flushing her lungs with pure oxygen, her heart rate picked up. Her rhythm was erratic with occasional runs of ventricular tachycardia (v-tach). The v-tach stopped shortly after, and her heart fell into a "livable" rhythm. She was still not breathing on her own, but I had that part under control for the time being. One of the other medics had already established a couple of IV lines, and we placed her on the stretcher and into the ambulance. One of the EMTs from the ladder company went to the hospital with the medics, and I stayed on scene. We did not know if this fire was a product of the arsonist that we had been chasing, but we couldn't count that out.

Are you ready for the twist? My wife and I took in a young boy in foster care about a year after that fire. He was a sad little fellow at first. Apparently, his mother and father had pretty much ignored him. The poor little guy was covered in scabies and lice. He didn't say much but would react positively to affection. We got him all cleaned up and well-fed. He started to talk and smile after a while. He was becoming a happy little fellow.

We had a small place at a nearby lake, and he loved going there and playing in the water. Both of my sons became very fond of having a little brother. Times were good.

My wife and I were watching TV one afternoon, and to our surprise, the arsonist who I had been chasing had been caught. They plastered his photo all over the TV, and he looked exactly like the little fellow that had been placed in our care. And then the ultimate fact that we could not escape, they had the same last name. There was no mistaking and no doubt at that time. The arsonist was our little guy's father.

The "coincidence" didn't stop there. We had been given the name of the boy's mother, and her name seemed very familiar to me. I did a bit of research and found that I had treated his mother medically several times. I knew his mother and now found his father had kept me up many nights on the job.

It gets even stranger, so now the BIG twist. The last name of the grandmother also sounded familiar and again I decided to do a bit more digging. The sixty-five-year-old house fire victim, who I had helped resuscitate, was the grandmother of the little fellow in our home. She had taken care of him after the house fire, which was, if you remember, about a year prior to our foster care.

As the famous American radio broadcaster Paul Harvey used to say, now for the rest of the story. After being in our care for almost two years, the boy ended up going back to the "care" of his mother, and then I heard later he was living with his aunt. We miss that little guy to this day. Foster care had encouraged us to let him call us "mommy" and "daddy" because there was no way he would ever be allowed to go back to his real family. We had intended to adopt him as soon as possible. One thing he had plenty of during the time he spent with us was love. To this day, I wish we had been allowed to give him the life he deserved, and which we could have given. Maybe a little selfish on my part, but then again, maybe not.

INCIDENT TWENTY-TWO:
"SPIRIT IN THE SKY"

Late one evening, our department received a call about a gasoline tanker that had crashed, resulting in a large fire on the side of the interstate highway. Two engine companies, a ladder company, a medic unit, a battalion chief, and an EMS captain were dispatched.

Engine-8 was first on the scene and reported a tractor trailer over the guardrail of the northbound side of the interstate at mile marker 171, with a large fire ball showing. Shortly thereafter, Ladder-1, Engine-1, Battalion Chief-1, and RS-1 arrived. Battalion 1 assumed command of the fire operations and requested Engine-7 and Heavy Tactical Rescue (HTR) 6 to also respond.

Engine-8 and Ladder-1 set up operations on the highway side of the scene, and Engine-1 was diverted to a street below the crash. When Engine-8 first arrived on the scene, the assumed driver was said to have been heard yelling and screaming for a few moments before he was not. There was absolutely no way for anyone to reach him in time. All we could settle with in our minds was that it didn't take very long.

Engine-7 became responsible for water supply and laid a five-inch line that supplied water to Ladder-1 and Engine-8. Engine-1 was able to hook into a hydrant on the lower street side operation. Medic-7 was assigned medical division, Medic-1 assisted Ladder-1, and HTR-6 stood by and assisted in fire operations.

That pretty much left me to wander and photograph the scene. I set up on a bridge overlooking the fire and started shooting photos. All of the shots were taken without the benefit of a tripod and are unfortunately blurred due to long exposure times.

The following photos pretty much speak for themselves. As we all knew a soul had been lost in that fire, I know several prayers were said for him and for his family. A solemn tone was maintained through the night.

After the fire was extinguished, the scene was turned over to the fire marshal, the state police, and the medical examiner's office.

INCIDENT TWENTY-THREE:
"CRIME REALLY DOESN'T PAY"

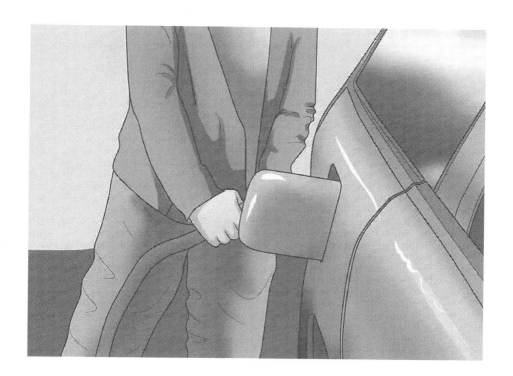

Many times, during one's career, one sees things that one cannot unsee. This incident is about one of those. When one thing initially goes wrong, the domino effect can, in fact, take over and control everything, regardless how it was intended.

We were called out for a structure fire with one known injury. The normal response was dispatched. Engine-8 (E-8), Engine-7 (E-7), Ladder-7 (L-7), Medic-8 (M-8), Battalion Chief-1 (BC-1), and Rescue Supervisor-1 (RS-1) responded to the scene. Upon our arrival, BC-1 assumed command as E-8 and L-7 took up positions for interior attack and ventilation. E-7 became responsible for water supply, and M-7 was the medical division. I was assigned to the rear of the structure, side-C, to act as the eyes and ears of BC-1, now referred to as incident command (IC). An additional medic unit, M-1, was dispatched to assist with the rapid intervention team (RIT), which had been initially created by two of the four firefighters from L-7.

As you can see, everyone had a specific job to perform, and the IC came up with the strategic plan, or strategy, and had everyone else perform the tactics to accomplish that goal.

As I rounded the rear of the house, I saw our patient sitting in the grass, holding his hand and in obvious pain from severe burns on his face, neck, arms, and chest. I immediately advised the IC and requested medical assistance to side-C.

The police always responded with us to structure fires and assisted in a multitude of ways. Usually, they would block or re-direct traffic away from the scene of the fire. They would make sure people didn't drive over our fire hoses, which would frequently look like large strands of spaghetti strung out on the roadway from the hydrant to the engine pumping the water to the other apparatus and in between the fire trucks and then on to the active fire scene itself.

On this occasion, I advised the IC what I saw on side-C, which consisted of an interesting twist to our fire scene. The patient indeed had severe burns and side-C was heavily involved with fire. I also requested the police and a fire marshal to join us.

It appeared that our patient was stealing fuel. He had a company truck up on jacks and running so the odometer on the vehicle continued to run. He also had "allegedly" placed a rubber hose into the vehicle's gas tank and ran the hose through an open basement door. Inside the door were several gas cans. According to the "victim," he was messing with the engine and his hand got caught up in the fan belt of the running engine. It avulsed several fingers and almost cut two of them completely off. Blood was all over the engine compartment. When his hand was injured, he fell backwards down the steps leading to the basement.

As he fell backwards, he tipped over one of the open gas cans and the gas spilled. Unfortunately for our patient, there happened to be a natural gas hot water heater in the basement. The fumes made their way to the pilot light and "KABOOM!!!" Karma strikes again.

While the firefighters were putting out the fire in our patient's house, the paramedics began treating the patient's hand injury and the burns from the explosion. The poor sucker's skin was literally dripping off his body.

They bandaged the man's hand and burns and placed him on the stretcher. As they were moving the strapped-in patient toward the ambulance, I heard one of the medics yell something like, "Oh! SHIT!" Then I turned to see the stretcher falling to one side. As the stretcher fell, the man's injured arm came out from the strap and slammed onto the pavement. The patient screamed out in agony. Just to make matters a bit worse, a fine representative of the local media was "Johnny-on-the-spot" and was filming as the stretcher toppled to the pavement.

I knew the reporter well, and we had been together at the scenes of many crimes, fires, and a multitude of various types of incidents over the years. I put my hand up to the camera lens and said," Please, for God's sake, don't publish that recording." Bless his heart, he did not. He let me view the tape the next day, so I could find out exactly why the stretcher had been dumped, along with the patient. It never did make it to the light of day. As far as I know, it was destroyed or simply taped over. One of the stretcher's wheels caught a piece of gravel and caused the stretcher to overturn. I did use that information to critique the unfortunate maneuver and try to make sure nothing like that happened again.

The gentleman in one fell swoop lost his job, almost burned his house down, and mangled his hand—not to mention the pain and scars from the flash burns. Oh, and did I mention he was charged with theft, and the fire marshal contemplated charging him with arson?

I suppose karma may really be a thing.

INCIDENT TWENTY-FOUR:
"UPSIDE DOWN"

When our EMS system merged with the city's fire department, like many others in the country, there was animosity within the ranks, and that animosity would sometimes rear its ugly head and create tension. Tension in the station was normally handled by the station officers and usually went no further. When the animosity showed up on an emergency scene, it would have to be dealt with on-the-spot and stopped when lives were at stake. This is one such situation of the latter.

Engine-6 (E-6), Medic-6 (M-6), Engine-5 (E-5) and Rescue Supervisor-1 (RS-1) responded to a motor vehicle accident with entrapment. E-6 and M-6 arrived simultaneously. The captain on E-6 appropriately stated on the radio, "Engine-6 arriving on scene of a single-vehicle motor vehicle accident with a pickup truck rollover." He gave the address and further commented, "E-6 assuming command and advised for E-5 and RS-1 to continue." A police officer arrived next, popped out a couple of flares, and then began blocking and diverting traffic. Traffic was light due to the early morning hour and the flares glowed bright red in the dark of night.

E-5 and I arrived at the same time and began assessing the scene. E-5 was the vehicle our department used for heavy rescue, such as vehicle extrication. My role at this point would be to direct the medical care of any victims.

Normally the engine company not involved directly with the patient's extrication would lay a charged water line to cover the men and women working to free the patients. This serves as fire prevention to protect the victims as well as the workers.

When I arrived on the scene, I saw a pickup truck situated in a very different position than any other I had seen in many years of experience. The truck had been traveling at a high rate of speed, even though this was a 25-m.p.h. speed zone. The driver apparently lost control, ran off the left side of the two-lane street, and struck a guidewire on a telephone pole. The truck traveled up the guidewire. I'm not sure exactly how high the truck ultimately traveled, but it rolled in the air and landed flat on the roof, resulting in the roof pancaking all the way to the frame of the doors on both sides.

There were two teenaged boys in the truck. We could hear at least one of them, but the only part of either occupant that was visible was part of the passenger's arm sticking out from under the collapsed roof.

E-5's personnel broke out their equipment, which were gasoline-powered hydraulic shears, spreaders, rams, and a combi-tool used for spreading and cutting.

Remember I mentioned the other engine normally laying out a charged water line? Well, I noticed it had not been done. The line was pulled but not charged. I casually mentioned to the incident commander, the captain from E-6, that we needed the line charged. Assuming he had simply forgotten, I fully expected him to order it done.

My attention was aimed more toward the patients and how we were going to be able to get them out of their extremely dangerous predicament. I looked back a few moments later to see the limp hose still laying on the street. This time I stated succinctly, "Captain, we need the line charged."

His reply was something like, "I'll do that when and if I think there is a need."

As the rest of the fire-EMS personnel were trying to save the lives of the two under the truck, the two of us had to argue about the water supply. I went to the captain of E-5 and advised that we did not yet have water supply, and he told his lieutenant to charge the line and it was done.

Once again, my attention went back to the trapped victims. The extrication started on the driver's side and from our contact with the driver, we found he still had a faint pulse but was unconscious and gravely injured. It did not look good for him at all. I advised that we had to go into triage mode. The extrication of the driver was going slowly due to the fact his legs were trapped under the dashboard and to get him out without further injury was going to take a great deal of time. We continued with the hydraulic rams and the cutter. I then advised the paramedic who was trying to treat the driver to let me know if he had lost a pulse. Within just a few minutes, the medic looked at me and shook his head. I ordered them to pull the driver out of the way so we could get to the passenger, who was still alive. We removed the driver and temporarily covered him with a sheet.

It was within our training and my experience of what to do when a trauma patient loses a pulse. The remote chance of resuscitation is 1 percent or less. Bottom line, it's not going to happen, and our attention needed to go to the patient who still had a chance at survival.

By rapidly removing the driver, it gave us much faster access to the viable patient. The driver was then considered a decedent rather than a patient.

The decedent turned out to be only seventeen years old and was, according to the police, at fault due to the high rate of travel.

The passenger was carefully extricated from the vehicle, and the paramedics from M-6 went to work. The patient was still conscious and was rapidly treated and transported to the nearest trauma center.

Postscript: The following day, I walked into the office of the deputy chief over operations and advised him of the verbal altercation on the accident scene. I also told the chief that the other captain and I circumvented the incident commander (the captain from E-6) in reference to the water supply. It is considered in extremely bad taste to ignore an order from the IC; however, in this case it was necessary due to the high risk of fire with a vehicle upside down, dumping gasoline and oil. The captain on E-6 was called into the office and issued a reprimand for unnecessarily risking the lives of the men and women on scene, as well as the patient, and for failure to follow department regulations.

The individuals for obvious reasons will remain anonymous.

INCIDENT TWENTY-FIVE:
"OUT ON A LIMB"

Sometimes acts of bravery are committed because the individual is or was brave. Usually, in my opinion, that is not really the case. Most of the time, I have found it to be rather out of necessity; it just turns out to leave the impression that the act itself was indeed brave. The following falls into that category.

Once again, the age-old preface appropriately applies; it *was a dark and stormy night*. It had been raining for a couple of days, rather hard at times. The rivers and creeks were all stretched just beyond capacity. The city's dispatcher had notified several of the fire-EMS officers as well as the police to visually monitor known areas of concern. This was an exercise we all had performed many times and usually to no major catastrophic outcome.

Apparently one of the low-lying streams had breached its banks and had covered a small bridge, in essence blocking the road. Keep in mind this was a remote area of the city and was not very heavily traveled. A railroad crossing was situated just prior to the road dropping off a bit and onto the then-water-covered bridge. Due to the rate of rainfall, the stream's current had increased exponentially.

A train had slowly approached the crossing and come to a stop. The engineer's concern had been the rising water. Keep in mind that a freaking train operator was worried about the rising water—a train! Well, here came not the brightest bulb in the chandelier. A person, according to the engineer, drove his car into the water not once, not twice, but three times trying to make it to the other side of the bridge that at that point was completely submerged, and the little stream had turned into a raging river.

This did not go well for the car or the driver. The car was swept up by the swift water and tossed up against a few small trees, just off the side of the road.

The car was precariously perched with its rear end wedged against the trees and water rushing all around the car. The driver was completely trapped.

The engineer called 9-1-1, and Ladder-2 (L-2), Engine-2 (E-2), Medic-2, Battalion Chief-2 (BC-2), and Rescue Supervisor-1 (RS-1) responded.

Upon our arrival, we found the scene as previously described. The water was up to the hood of the car. The doors were also covered up. The little stream—now river—had large things floating downstream that would occasionally hit the front of the car. The trees were swaying with the current, and we literally studied the scene and tried to come up with a safe way to extricate the gentleman from his self-imposed predicament.

The car was too far to reach with a rope or a throw bag, and our system did not at that time have a swift water rescue team. They would have definitely come in handy.

The following is what these well-trained, intelligent officers decided to do to solve this complex problem. The ladder truck was positioned on and parallel to the tracks. The dispatcher notified the railroad company of the situation and that the tracks would be blocked for an unknown amount of time. The truck's ladder was extended as far as it could be, and ground ladders were used to try and stabilize it. Keep in mind, the ladder on that truck was not really made to be extended out to the side—upward and at an angle, yes, but not straight out to the side.

To this day, I'm not exactly sure how or why I was selected to go out on the ladder, but it doesn't really matter. Like a good little rescuer, I donned my rappelling gear and ropes. I took along some extra two-inch webbing as well to secure the driver. So here I go crawling optimistically but slowly along the outstretched ladder, illuminated not only by the lights from our equipment but also from the media that had just arrived. Audie, the captain from E-2, followed me up and out onto the ladder. He also had on repelling gear and a safety line attached to the ladder itself. The plan was for me to exit the extended ladder and rappel down to the car. Audie brought with him a handheld windshield saw so I could access the occupant. He also brought a ground ladder to be attached to the end of the truck's extended arm to help bring the driver out and up to safety.

The lieutenant in charge of L-2 advised me not to bounce at the end of the ladder. He basically stated the ladder might at that point dump me, Audie, and the truck's outstretched ladder into the river. Those, let me tell you, were NOT comforting words to hear.

I did not know Audie well at this point in our careers, but we would end up working closely together for the entire balance of our time with the city as well as in the medical examiner's office as investigators.

Later, we were able to laugh about what happened next on the ladder but, at the time, not so much.

Audie accidentally dropped the windshield saw into the water as I was just about to drop off the end of the ladder. I remember trying to keep my knees on the last rung, but then they slipped, and I felt my weight load the rope and the ladder did what they told me not to let it do. It bounced. I waited a moment expecting Humpty Dumpty to fall off the wall, but thank God, Humpty was dangling but not falling. Unfortunately, there was something else that went wrong as I came off the end of the ladder. I was holding onto the second rung of the ladder and my elbow took on my body weight as I slipped, and it dislocated. I saw it pop out and then back in. Yes sir, that hurt. Then dangling, I slowly lowered myself onto the hood of the nearly submerged car.

I still needed to breach the windshield to access the then-frantic occupant. Believe it or not, he was trying to open the door and was yelling, with a tone reminiscent of Foster Brooks, "Just give me a push, and I can drive out." He was even trying to restart the engine. Audie lowered a fire axe from the end of the ladder, and I told the obviously inebriated want-to-be driver to get back from the windshield and to cover his face and head. He held his hands up and pleaded with me to not break the glass. I did not oblige.

This photo is from the local newspaper.

I struck the glass with the pointed edge of the axe and broke through. Remember, I had just dislocated my left elbow. I had no choice but to continue the best way I could. As I was trying to cut through the glass, Audie was busy securing the ground ladder he had brought with him to the end of the extended ladder from the truck.

In the meantime, trees and all sorts of stuff continued floating down the river and hitting the front of the car. So long as the ladder truck's appendage did not fail, I felt comfortable having a safety line tied off to the ladder from which I had dropped.

Back to the man in the car. The water was up to his chest, and he realized I was going to extract him from his precarious position through the hole in the windshield. I finally got most of his torso through the windshield and tied a "hasty hitch" on him and attached the hitch to my harness. Then, in essence, we were both secured to the ladder above.

I helped him out of the car and onto the wet, slippery hood. His breath was that of a drunken sailor, and the comments that were exchanged were similar. He kept complaining that I broke his damn windshield, and I simply told him to shut the fuck up! My patience was rather thin at that moment.

Audie had since secured the ground ladder and dropped another line to attach to our idiot. I took a carabiner and clipped it though a couple of the loops on the subject's hitch and then to the rope dangling from above. That way Audie could pull from above and I could push from below. I then unhooked the carabiner from my harness, freeing me from his hitch. It was a bit awkward trying to get him up and onto the truck's main ladder, but after a lot of tugging and pushing we made it.

I stayed on the hood of the car until Audie crawled back with the man to the fire truck's turntable and handed him off to the personnel still on dry land. After they cleared the ladder, I slowly climbed back up and off to safety.

As soon as I reached the shore, I located the nearest police officer and advised that the man had tried several times to start the car, and the next thing I saw was a shiny pair of bracelets encompassing my newfound friend's wrists, which were conveniently now behind his back.

I then walked over to the medic unit and told them I needed to go to the emergency department to have my elbow examined. So, the dummy from the car went to jail for DUI, and Humpty Dumpty ended up at the hospital for most of the rest of the shift.

Audie went back to the scene the next day. The water had subsided, and he found the windshield saw.

Audie and I had many adventures together over the span of about sixteen years and became exceptionally good friends.

INCIDENT TWENTY-SIX:
"GET THE BUCK OFF MY TRUCK"

Occasionally, fire-EMS and the police will encounter something they have never seen before, and, quite frankly, those times are few and far between. This is most certainly one of those occurrences.

I was driving back from a call on the north side of the city at zero dark hundred hours one morning when a police code 10-50 PI (vehicle accident with personal injury) rang out on the radio. I made a quick turnaround, flipped on my emergency lights, and hit the siren. The weather was clear but with a chill in the air. I was tired as usual at that time of the night, but onward I trudged.

On many occasions, a vehicle accident would go out over the air and either PD, an engine company, or even an ambulance would arrive prior to my entry on the scene, and they would cancel me due to the fact it was minor and something they could handle. This time, however, I arrived before anyone else to something that at first did not make any sense.

I marked on scene to the accident and reported that apparently only one vehicle was involved. Sometimes, we would encounter a single-vehicle accident, and the other vehicle fled the scene before we arrived—normally because of an outstanding warrant or maybe they were drunk and trying to avoid a DUI.

A pickup truck was pulled over in the emergency lane on the northbound side of the interstate that ran through the city. I pulled in behind the pickup truck, and I could see two subjects still sitting in the truck. Steam or smoke was rising from the front of the vehicle, and I also noted what appeared to be broken glass scattered about, behind, and to the side of the truck.

Our training was remarkably similar to that of the police when encountering a vehicle on the side of the road. That position is extremely dangerous with cars and trucks flying by. I pulled my SUV within about ten feet from the rear of the pickup and angled the front of my vehicle to the left of the pickup to block traffic from where I was about to exit my unit. Keep in mind, my emergency lights were still flashing, and the white strobes cut through the darkness like a knife through butter. They could be seen from a long distance. By the way, one other reason we were taught to angle our unit in that way was to give the first responder immediate cover if the occupants of the pickup were to come out and attack for any reason. One would retreat placing the engine block between the attackers and the responder. Hopefully, my vehicle would take a bullet instead of me.

I stepped out onto the side of the road and slowly approached the driver's side of the pickup. All the while, I was interested in seeing the driver's hands and making sure nothing was being held that could be used as a weapon. It was a crew cab, so as I approached, I paused to shine a flashlight into the rear seating area, which was also part of our training. I noticed more broken glass in the rear seat and what appeared to be good deal of blood. I could see the driver's hands were empty as well as the passenger's. I also saw that most of the windshield was broken and bloody.

I asked, "What the hell happened?" The driver exclaimed, "We were attacked by a damn buck!" Both men in the pickup were covered with blood and I tried to put two-and-two together but kept getting three or maybe five. I felt like it was a dumb question, but I asked if they were OK. The response was, "Scared half to death and cut up a bit." I reiterated, "What the hell happened?" The driver said to look at the front of the truck. I walked around and the right front of the truck was banged up a little and a headlight was knocked out. I quickly found the culprit lying dead under the right front wheel. If memory served, it was an eight-point buck. A rather nice sized specimen he was. It kind of started to make some sense, but I still did not quite understand the windshield or all the glass and blood in the truck.

The buck had jumped just as the truck was about to hit him and landed square on the windshield, imploding the glass into the truck and onto the occupants. The blow from the collision, as the men put it, "Didn't hurt that damn thing at all." The frightened deer began kicking and biting and goring the men, and they in turn fought off the mad animal with Herculean strength brought about by, I'm sure, one hell of a rush of adrenaline. They pushed the attacker back through the windshield, and as the buck dropped to the pavement, the driver quickly accelerated bringing a halt to the white-tailed wonder's life.

The next thing I saw was Medic-2, Engine-2, and a police car approaching. They arrived and I filled them in on what had just transpired. A few chuckles were heard, hopefully not by the men involved in the incident. They were both treated for minor injuries, and the pickup truck had to be towed off. The driver made a cell phone call, and a friend came by to give them a lift. The buck was transported by the city to the dump, never to be seen again.

You must realize, those two guys have one of the best deer stories ever.

INCIDENT TWENTY-SEVEN:
"RATS, RATS, RATS"

I am not exactly sure how or where to start this one. I wish I could say it was a dark and stormy night, but, well, it was not. It was a beautiful bright sunny day in our fair city, and I had just finished my lunch. I remember topping it off with an ice cream cone. Why I remember that fact is beyond me, but there it is. Sarah and I—I told you, you would hear more about Sarah—were just sitting around the station watching TV. This time of day, Sarah took guard of the TV remote control. It was one of the old box TVs, long before the invention of flat screens. As I noted earlier, she was about ten years older than me, as reminded me quite often. She loved her soaps in the early afternoon and fighting with her over the channel changer was futile.

Sarah was a slightly heavyset, short, black lady and one of the finest human beings I have ever had the privilege to know and with whom to work. She would show up to the crew hall like clockwork in her blue slacks and white shirt adorned with a silver badge marked with an EMS star of life and a lieutenant's bar. The shirt also had lieutenant's bars on both epaulets. She was the extremely proud 1st lieutenant of one of the volunteer crews that the city career medics were helping to cover 9-1-1 calls. She had definite opinions on absolutely everything and had zero hesitancy in expressing said opinions. I have traveled just a tad off track, but you really did need to hear more about Sarah. We forged a friendship I will remember to my grave.

Back to the not-so dark and stormy night/day. We received a call for a woman down in her home and in need of assistance. Sarah climbed into the driver's seat, and I jumped in the passenger's seat. I picked up the microphone and advised dispatch that we were en route to the residence and gave the address. Sarah flipped on the red lights and siren, and we were off. The amount of time to arrive was truly minimal, just a few minutes. I announced on the radio of our presence on the scene and we both exited the ambulance with its red lights still flashing.

We were told by the dispatcher that the lady in distress wanted us to enter from the back porch and that we could come in on our arrival. Sarah and I walked onto the back porch to find millions of sunflower seeds under foot. There was absolutely no way one could place one's foot on the porch without crunching the seeds. I swear they were several inches deep. I remember a little rock wall acting as a retainer for the yard, which was level with the top of the wall. Out of the corner of my eyes, I kept thinking that I saw something move within the gaps of stone in the wall. I mentioned it to Sarah, and then we knocked on the door as we entered the home and announced, "City EMS"! We're coming in! City EMS!"

OK, here we are crunching our way into the living room to see, you guessed it, rats, rats, and more RATS!!! Absolutely everywhere!!! I thought we were in the middle of the Pied Piper's movie. Did I mention that I have one major phobia? Well, let me tell you now, I am terrified of freaking RATS! They were everywhere. On the chairs, on the sofa, all over the floor, climbing on all the furniture and running, apparently not knowing I was much more afraid than they were. The odor as we entered hit you like a brick shithouse. With that said, I sucked it up and turned my attention at first to a single neurotic cat sitting on the back of the sofa. The cat looked as terrified as I am sure I did. Sarah, on the other hand, seemed to take the infestation with a grain of salt, and we crunched our way into the next room to find the person in need of our assistance.

Our patient was a little old lady on her knees in a doorway leading to the kitchen. Her grey hair was disheveled, and her filthy dress was up around her waist. The smell of rat, cat, and human urine and feces permeated the house. Another lady was standing nearby in tears. The poor woman on the floor had rats all around her and on her. As we advanced toward the patient, the rats scurried away. The poor lady's legs were covered in blood from none other than rat bites. Her lower legs were blue from lack of circulation. She had bites all over her arms, legs, feet, and even some on her neck. She advised that she had been on the floor for two days prior to the 9-1-1 call. The other woman in the room was the patient's sister, and they lived in this home together. As we started treating the partially eaten woman, I asked the sister when she had found her sister on the floor. The reply sent chills through my body, and Sarah and I could only look at each other in horror. She said she had been with her the entire time and had finally decided to call for help. I then asked, I am certain with a scolding tone, "Why did you wait so long?" She said, "They're our babies, they're our pets. We were afraid you would take them away." All the seeds on the porch and in the house had been put there by the women to feed their "pets."

We extricated both deranged ladies from their rat house and placed them in the back of the ambulance. Sarah stayed with the two women, and I keyed my mic and advised dispatch that we needed animal control posthaste. I felt like calling in an airstrike on the residence. My God in heaven, I had never seen anything like that and pray never to again.

We transported the women to the hospital, and the doctors alerted adult protective services (APS) that their assistance was required at the hospital's emergency department. There was no way in hell those ladies were going to be allowed back in that house. The patient's wounds were attended to, and she was given shots for everything they could come up with, including rabies, I am sure. They were both held in the emergency department until APS took over responsibility for the women. They were both eventually placed in a nursing home, courtesy of the city.

To see what had happened to the pesky little critters, that to this day still give me a major case of the heebie-jeebies, I drove back by the house several days later. I saw a multitude of people from the city's health department, animal control, and sanitation department in and around the house. The house had been condemned, and there were at least fifty large garbage bags full of dead rats. A few days later the house had been knocked down and taken away, leaving just a foundation and that little rock wall. I was afraid to walk over and look at the wall just in case they had missed a few rats. Just thinking about that house and that poor lady on the floor still makes my skin crawl.

INCIDENT TWENTY-EIGHT:
"YOU WANT SOME OF THIS?"

How does that old saying go, "Life imitates art," or is it "Art imitates life?" Whichever it is, this next incident reminds me of a carnival knife-throwing act that did not really end very well.

While doing my daily rounds from station to station, a call went out for a man knocking on a lady's door requesting assistance. The man apparently had been knocking on several doors trying to get someone to answer his plea for help. Not that he really needed much, facetiously I speak.

The man had already walked away from the address we were given over the radio, so we had to hunt a little bit to find the gentleman in distress. The last person who saw him walking down the street advised that it appeared he had a knife sticking in his face.

On occasion, callers would give us descriptions that were generally accurate to what occurred. Then again, sometimes their descriptions were right on the nose. Pun intended. I drove around the block a couple of times until I noticed a man sitting on the front steps of a house close to the original caller. I pulled over and advised dispatch I was on scene and for the medic unit to step it up.

I rarely asked for a unit to hurry, knowing full well they would get there as soon as they could, but this time...well, let me describe what I found as I walked up to the patient. The man was sitting by himself on the front concrete steps of an old white house with large round wooden columns. The house was in slight disrepair, perfectly framing the subject. With both hands wrapped around the knife handle, he was pulling as hard as he could to dislodge the kitchen knife from his nose.

The first thing that came to mind, which I blurted out, was "Oh shit, dude, stop doing that. I'm an old paramedic and you're going to make ME sick."

When I first approached him, I could smell the distinct odor of alcohol on his breath. As a matter of fact, he reeked. He looked at me with the knife sticking out of his left nostril and exclaimed, "Will you pull this damn thing out, it's killing me." I guarantee, had it not been a profoundly serious-looking injury, I would have laughed my ass off.

I told him we would take care of it and to quit pulling on the knife. The medic unit arrived, and we finally got the fella settled down and bandaged the knife in place with a "doughnut roll," which was just thick bandages wrapped around the knife and his head until the knife was completely stable. We then secured him to the stretcher so he could hardly move and definitely could not grab the knife and try to pull it out again. The medic unit transported our patient to the hospital, and I followed in my response unit.

Upon arrival to the ED, the patient was wheeled into the trauma room, and the guy was still making wisecracks.

Everyone who has ever worked in or around a hospital ED has heard pretty much everything that can be uttered by an extremely inebriated human being. This guy, however, took the cake. After they had x-rayed his head and removed the bandages, they were talking of sending him to surgery. The patient with a knife handle sticking out of the middle of his face tried to grab one of the nurse's butts and, looking similar to Jimmy Durante doing a ha-cha-cha-cha routine, said, "Hey baby, you want some of this?" The answer was a resounding, "Not on your life. buster."

The following is a photo of an actual x-ray taken in the ED that day. The doctor wanted a copy and so did I. The name of the "gentleman" is obviously left out.

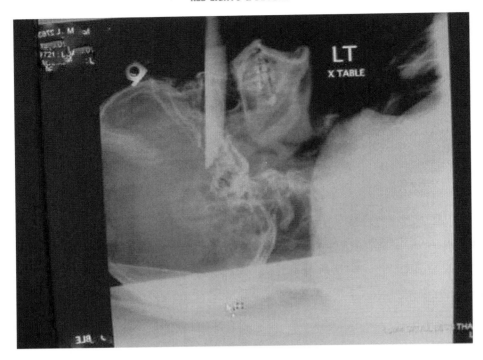

I understand that the blade tip did not make it into the brain cavity, but he probably had a runny nose for a few days.

INCIDENT TWENTY-NINE:
"BACK-TO-BACK"

I really should have combined these two stories since they are extremely short and have very similar outcomes.

Once again, I was driving around town doing my normal thing when a call went out for a fight with a man down. Generally, when I know violence is involved, I would hold back for the police to go in and secure the scene. This time, as I rounded a blind corner from a stop sign, the address given out for the call was directly in front of me, and several people were waving at me to come and help. Had I decided not to go in and wait for PD, the subjects involved would have probably been pushed into an adversarial relationship when I did move in with the ambulance and police.

I assessed the scene as best as I could and elected to go in. To help you visualize the area, it was mid-morning, about ten-hundred hours, in a residential area of the city. Small, old homes lined the streets, with an occasional empty lot and a corner store and bar nearby. The weather was clear and not a factor. I saw about five or six black males, guessed to be in their late teens to early twenties motioning to me for help. At that point I had no idea what had happened or to whom it had happened. I advised dispatch I was on scene and gave her the address. I exited my vehicle to find one young man sitting on the curb with everyone else standing and simply gazing at the soon-to-be patient. I stood directly in front of the subject and noticed a look of desperation along with the fact he was profusely sweating and extremely pale, almost ashen in skin color. I asked him what had happened, and he told me he and a "friend" had gotten into an argument and right before the "friend" ran off, the young man stated, "He hit me in the fucking back."

Being the overly intelligent sleuth that I am, that gave me cause to observe the patient's back. I gave him a double take and said, "Yep, he hit you in the back alright, and we have proof—and probably fingerprints." The patient did not yet know he had a knife sticking out of his back. It turned out to be a folding knife with a four-inch blade buried all the way to the hilt. I found it hard to believe, but the others had not informed the young man of his true predicament.

I obliged and simply stated, "You have a knife stuck into your back, remarkably close to your spine. Please do not move a muscle. The ambulance will be here momentarily, and I am going to sit behind you and help you stay very, very still."

I heard the medic unit and the fire truck's sirens coming closer and closer until they rounded the corner. Medic-9 and Engine-9 had extremely seasoned medics and EMTs on board, and after they arrived, I turned the patient over to them. I had obtained minimal information other than that he was obviously getting shocky and was in serious condition. I was able to obtain a carotid pulse, but the radial was absent. His blood pressure was estimated to be approximately sixty systolic, and his respiratory rate was considerably shallow and elevated. I suspected a punctured lung at the very least. The paramedics from Medic-9 bandaged and stabilized the knife in place with a "doughnut roll." The patient had good feeling in all extremities and was able to move his fingers and toes. Everything seemed to be functional. The patient was then loaded onto the stretcher face down. We rarely transported a patient in the prone position, but for obvious reasons this time we did.

The fortunate young man did well en route to the hospital. His vitals remained stable, and he remained alert and oriented.

After he was transferred to the hospital, he continued to talk about getting that "SOB back for this shit."

In the hospital after the bandage was removed, I took a better look at the handle and noticed it had a Harley-Davidson insignia. I asked the ED doc if he wanted a photo, and his reply was "Hell, yes."

The following photos are from that day in the ED. I gave a copy to the doctor.

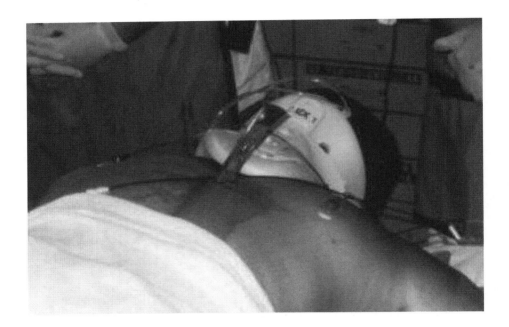

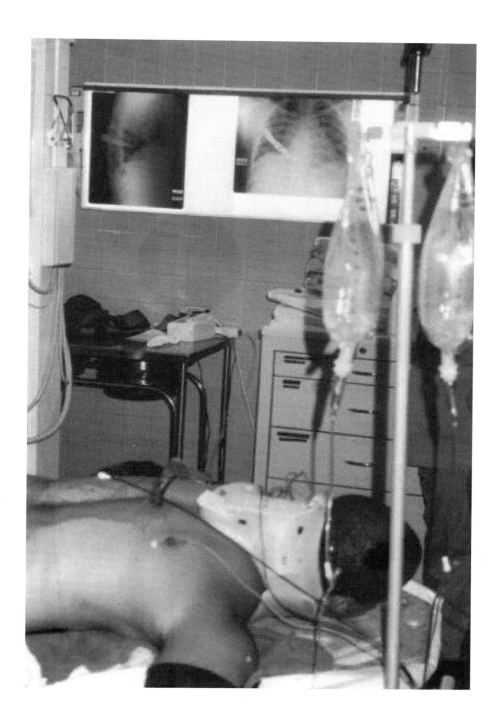

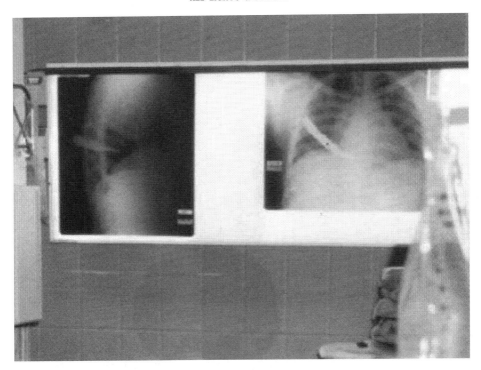

The knife missed all his vital organs and the patient recovered. I never heard anything about any retaliation, but I would be surprised if the knife-wielding subject did not get stuck or shot later. Just seemed to be the way things went.

INCIDENT THIRTY:
"FIRE AND ICE"

If you remember, I mentioned that I had started out running with a volunteer fire department and ended up showing more interest in the world of emergency medical services (EMS). Keep in mind, I did not mind fighting fire, it just was not my forte, plus it had been quite a while since I had really applied much effort toward training on the fire side. Well, when the two departments decided to merge, and, by the way, I thought it was a great idea to do so, I continued my fire training along with EMS continuing education.

Let me back up just a bit. Our city, as I have said, had three emergency service departments: police, fire, and EMS. Police and fire had been long-established departments, and EMS was truly an infant. We all got along well until the city decided it was no longer cost effective to keep them all separate. At one point, the thought was bounced around about a public safety department encompassing all three. Police officers responding to fire and EMS calls to possibly fight fires and perform CPR, as well as fire and EMS personnel responding with pistols and shotguns in hand to public safety calls. This was finally dumped, and the process started to get more serious. The city formed a "strategic planning" group with a "project management team."

The project management team was to be led by the director of public safety and consist of five additional personnel from city administration, four officers from the fire department, four officers from city EMS, two officials from the volunteer EMS system, and the city's operational medical director. Being one of three EMS supervisors, and due to the fact, I had voiced my interest in a fire-EMS department, I was requested to participate.

This entire process took approximately two years and was the mother and father of many years of growing pains for all personnel involved.

At first, the traditional fire guys did not want to run EMS calls. Most of the EMS personnel were on board, but there were a few holdouts that did not want to fight fires. Saying that there was animosity would be a gross understatement. My role as one of three EMS supervisors turned into being an EMS operations captain with the newly formed fire-EMS Department. The three of us were placed on several different committees and given the appearance of a step above that of a fire captain. We were responsible for all EMS operations citywide on our shift, as well as office responsibilities, such as employee evaluations for all EMS personnel on our shift. In addition, we were to respond to and participate in fire side operations.

I personally developed the city's EMS peer review and assigned personnel on a rotation to the committee. The EMS personnel were used to being critiqued by their peers; however, the fire side really got their backs up when it came to criticism. Unfortunately, this seemed to create more animosity between the two groups. It appeared to be a necessary evil at the time. Speaking of time, that was the only sure remedy for the painful transition within the two departments. After so many years, the new employees going through the fire-EMS academy had been trained in both disciplines and came out into the field aware of their responsibilities. Complaints decreased and the two babies finally grew up. Like us old, retired fire-EMS folks do on occasion, I have run rather far off the base line and need to get back to running the bases and work my way back to home plate.

What was the name of this incident? Oh yeah, I remember, "Fire and Ice."

Winter in our fair little city could at times be rather brutal for those of us having to work out of doors. This incident was at least that, if not much, much worse.

We were called for a fire in a warehouse just north of city center. The first alarm went out, and the dispatcher called for Engine-3, Medic-3, Engine-5, Ladder-2, Medic-2, Battalion Chief-2, and RS-1 to respond. As the first units arrived, it was announced over the radio that they had a three-story brick warehouse with fire and smoke showing from sides A and B. Battalion Chief-2 arrived shortly thereafter and called for a second alarm. The deputy chief over operations also responded. The second alarm brought in Engine-9, Medic-9, Engine-1, and Ladder-1. Battalion Chief-1 also responded.

It was very, very cold that day, and everything that was touched by water, if it was not on fire, turned to ice. Firefighters were sliding around like a bunch of clowns in an ice rink show. Footing was extremely difficult. We had to get one of the city's salt trucks to bring salt in to assist.

When the call initially came out, I was about as far away from that address as I could get and still be in the city limits. By the time I arrived, the deputy chief had taken over command of the fire scene and called for a third alarm. Several additional apparatuses responded. I reported to command and asked what he needed me to do. That may have been a mistake, knowing full well that most of the fire ground positions I would normally take or be assigned were already being covered. He said, "Pack up and take a line and assist Ladder 1 on the roof." My response was, "Copy Chief."

As I was donning my turnout gear and MSA air pack, I mumbled to myself, "Hell, that is going to really suck." I had to climb a ground ladder to the first-floor roof and then another ladder from that roof to the top of the third-floor roof. Keep in mind I had on about sixty pounds of gear plus the two-and-a-half-inch line over my shoulder and not to mention ice, ICE, EVERYWHERE! The ladder leading to the top of the building was extremely shaky, and another firefighter steadied it as I climbed up.

Once at the top, I climbed over the parapet wall onto the roof. I had to walk across about sixty feet of flat roof to another brick wall extending several feet high, forming the top of a "fire wall." On the other side of the fire wall, there were flames sixty to eighty feet high with dark smoke shooting hundreds of feet toward the sky. The roof on the other side of the fire wall was melting and some parts had already collapsed. I heard an explosion of some type and looked to my right to see a firefighter tethered to the top of the ladder truck's extended ladder being whipped, violently back and forth over the street below. Pieces of the ladder's water pipe fell, landing around the men and women fighting the fire from the street level. The hard pipe that runs the length of the ladder had literally blown apart. The force it took to whip that ladder around was enormous. The firefighter at the top was no worse for wear from his carnival ride, and miraculously, no one on the ground was hit by the falling debris.

As the fire continued to burn out of control, we eventually had to retreat from the roof, back down the ladders. The interior group that had been attacking the fire from within, the building on which I had been standing, also retreated. At that time, the order was given to simply pour as much water as we could on the fire and go to a surround and drown attack.

Eventually all fires go out. Either the amount of water cools the fuel, or it simply runs out of something to burn. I am not sure who won that war, but the building was definitely a complete loss. I remember returning to the site a couple of months later to see an empty lot where the once-stately brick building had stood. Every time I think of that fire, I remember how damn cold it was on the ground and how ridiculously hot it was on the roof.

Lesson learned. If you know you are not going to like the answer, do not be stupid and ask the question.

These photos of the fire were taken by the local newspaper.

INCIDENT THIRTY-ONE:
"DEAD END"

As I have alluded to, working with the state medical examiner's (ME) office offered up a great number of unfortunate if not strange cases. Humor was used at many death scenes as a coping mechanism. I have heard an untold number of EMS personnel, police, as well as death investigators make totally inappropriate jokes over a dead body—I might add, never when family or friends or another human being not in the job happened to be around. It just seemed to be the way things were.

Normal people are just not confronted daily with death, dying, and destruction. For example, I remember hearing a medic, while searching for bodies and body parts in the rubble of a fire and building collapse, yell out, "Can anybody give me a hand?" The answer pierced the air as if an arrow had traversed the scene; it was "No, but I found how I can get a head." Body parts were gradually found as a large track hoe slowly and methodically scratched the burned wood and scorched concrete, brick, and whatever else was left of the building and its contents.

I really believe if humor had not been allowed or accepted, we all would have lost our minds. The unfortunate thing is that some of us did. Suicide was not an everyday event, but it certainly was not unheard of among first responders. More about that later.

I seem to continue to wander around in my head when trying to convey how normal people deal with abnormal situations. We were not superhuman. We were just a bunch of type-A personalities that elected to go into public service of one sort or another and had to figure out our own way to cope.

This case came into the medical examiner's office as a body found at the end of a closed-off street. The typical signage was placed near the blocked-off roadway. Another road had been put in place several years ago, which made this one null and void.

I reiterate, humor at times just seemed appropriate, and it would occasionally just roll off one's tongue before it could be stopped. The police had been on scene for an hour or so before they even notified the ME's office. The call was in the city, and the officers on scene were all familiar with my prior employment as a fire-EMS Captain. When I arrived, a sergeant who will remain unnamed yelled out between chuckles, "No, NO, Pope. Don't do it, it's too late." He was referring to me not attempting to resuscitate this unfortunate homeless man.

To make matters even worse, the poor soul was lying face down at the base of one of the signs. You guessed it, the sign said, "DEAD END."

After I placed my little evidence ruler down beside the body, with a case number and my initials written upon it, I started taking photographs, and I could not resist the temptation to make sure the Dead-End sign was included in as many of the photos as possible.

Jokes were flying back and forth between the police and myself. I am not sure how many dead-end jokes there are, but let it suffice to say, there were many. "I guess he could not run any further—he came to a dead end." "I guess the guy lost his promotion and had a dead-end job." By the way, none of these pseudo-jokes were funny; they were simply, as I stated, helping us cope with the incredibly sad end of a life. No one was probably even going to claim the body.

I finished my routine of photographing at first the scene and then the body. After I finished shooting him in the position found, I rolled him over and continued to shoot. The police investigator could then complete his required photography, as well. We found nothing remarkable—no gunshot wounds, no puncture wounds that could be made by a knife. Nothing to show any type of trauma to the head or body other than multiple animal bites that all appeared to be postmortem. The assumption was he had probably died from natural causes or possibly a drug or alcohol overdose.

We also found a letter with a name and address. The police would soon follow up on that information, but other than the letter, no identification was found on his person. I placed a "John Doe" toe tag on his big toe by wrapping the attached wire around the toe. We then rolled the body into the opened body bag I had placed beside the unfortunate man. I then made out another tag with the same information and attached it to the bag itself. The officers kindly assisted me with loading the body onto a stretcher and into the nondescript white van I had driven to the scene.

I said my goodbyes, thanked the officers, and went on my merry way. When I arrived at the office, I drove around back where the intake cooler was located. I removed the stretcher from the van and escorted the gentleman to his temporary resting place. With a slight push, the door slammed shut on the cage now containing the body. Once closed and locked, the chain of evidence would be maintained, and the next time the cage would be opened would be the next morning by the autopsy technician. The body would either be viewed by one of the pathologists or given a full autopsy. Probably an autopsy.

Sad, but oh so true. This type of incident was not uncommon at all.

INCIDENT THIRTY-TWO:
"BONES"

When I joined the Office of the Chief Medical Examiner (OCME) as a medicolegal death investigator (D-ABMDI), I assumed I would encounter situations that would be, well, different from what I had dealt with in EMS. In fact, a lot of the cases I worked on as an investigator were quite similar. I was intimately familiar with death, and I was used to odd circumstances. I had never, however, dug up a bunch of bones and tried to figure out to whom they belonged and how the individual had died.

I was working a daylight shift at the OCME, and the chief forensic pathologist said that one of the forensic anthropologists was not able to respond to the scene of some human remains and that she needed me to accompany the one who could. The remains had been discovered by a dog. The dog brought one of the upper arm bones to its owner's home, and the owner called 9-1-1, recognizing the bone was that of a human.

We had a bone sent to our office one time, and the local ME had looked at it and forwarded it to us. I opened the box and within seconds recognized it as that of a pig. The chief forensic pathologist concurred, and the case was, as they say, closed.

I met the forensic anthropologist at the crime scene, which had been cordoned off by the police, once again in the city where I had previously worked as a fire-EMS captain. And again, the jokes were rampant. "No, Pope, do not do it...No, Pope, it's too late." I let most of them go, but when one sergeant said, "If you try to resuscitate this decedent, I will shoot you." My response was, "If you shoot me, you will be in a lot of trouble and generate a hell of a lot of paperwork, asshole. Plus, you will not have anyone to dig up the bones."

He then retreated, and I started to work with one of the most amazing individuals I have ever had the honor to work with.

Luckily, the police at least had a clue who the person who had previously occupied the discovered bones might be. Reportedly an elderly lady, who apparently did not have a good sense of direction, had wondered off into the woods and sat down on a log. That was the last position the person had taken with knowledge of their surroundings.

Dr. Dickerson and his wife normally worked together on this type of situation, but she was slightly ill and had stayed home. It turned out that I would be incredibly grateful to fill her place.

We brought a large number of different-sized brown paper bags, a couple of black permanent markers, evidence tape, evidence rulers, string, and wooden stakes along with a mallet to drive the stakes. The forensic anthropologist had been through the drill many times. As for my experience with the upcoming procedures—none, other than a summer job digging up and transplanting graves for the Kentucky highway department when I was only seventeen. I had to either follow his lead or just listen and ask questions. I am sure he got tired of all the questions, but he had the patience of Job.

We began by making a grid on paper and then on the ground with wooden stakes and string around the discovered bones. Once bones are discovered and determined to be human remains, the police as well as the OCME's office become involved.

We would find a small piece of bone, which Dr. Dickerson was quickly able to recognize. I would photograph the piece next to an evidence ruler labeled with the case number and my initials. It was then carefully removed from its resting place and deposited into one of the brown paper bags. The bag was then labeled with a black permanent marker and sealed with evidence tape.

The bags were all lined up next to the site, and at that point everything started to make sense.

We meticulously removed pieces of this poor lady's body and put them in paper bags. This process continued until either we uncovered all the remains, or it got too dark to work. It took us two days to recover everything we could. We even used a camera capable of being run up a hole in a tree trunk or down a hole in the ground to see if animals had carried off some of the decedent's missing bones.

After collecting everything we possibly could, we took all the bags of bones back to the OCME and unpacked them. All the pieces and parts were put back together on a stainless-steel table like a jigsaw puzzle. It was amazing how the anatomy of the human body revealed itself and revealed the probable cause of death. In this case, there were no unusual marks or stressors on the bones. It was determined that she had more than likely wandered off into the woods and died of exposure to the elements. The decedent was identified utilizing mitochondrial DNA. She was found to have had a history of Alzheimer's and that probably contributed greatly to the incident.

I had the opportunity to work two separate cases with Dr. Dickerson and both were as intriguing as anything I had ever done.

A human skull could be sent to the FBI laboratory, and they could reconstruct the physical features of the person. A missing person poster would be generated and circulated throughout all the police and sheriff's departments nationwide. We had four such missing person cases in our office, and two of the people were identified during the four years I spent with the department. Real science is truly more amazing than fiction.

INCIDENT THIRTY-THREE:
"NURSING HOME HEALTH CARE IS AN OXYMORON"

Full disclosure, I have been in every nursing home in the city and surrounding area, and I have not found one that provides good-to-excellent health care. I do not think it is completely the fault of the employees as much as the owner/operators. The nursing homes are almost always understaffed, which in turn makes the employees overworked. This, however, I do not consider justification for totally inept nurses and/or nurse's aides.

Do not get me wrong—I very highly respect the nursing profession. I have had the honor to work with some of the most knowledgeable and well-trained nurses over the years. I have learned an unbelievable amount of medical knowledge and techniques from some of the most professional nurses out there. With that said, they did not work in a nursing home.

For example, we were called to an unnamed nursing home one evening for a "code blue" with CPR in progress. I walked into the room and immediately asked the nurse's aide (NA), who was by herself, to discontinue CPR, and I checked the poor old dead guy for a pulse. As soon as I touched him, I knew he had been dead for quite a while. I looked at the NA (who was still the only one in the room other than myself) with my arms and hands spread out in a gesture of question, and she said, "I saw him take his last breath and immediately started CPR and had the charge nurse call 9-1-1." The EMS crew as well as the engine company had already arrived, and I told them to clear up and that I would take care of the situation and the paperwork.

I looked back at the NA and said, "This man has been dead for at least an hour or two, maybe more." She replied, with a snippy attitude, "That's impossible!" I asked her to call her supervisor to the room. The supervisor was a registered nurse (RN).

When the supervisor arrived, I asked her to look at the man's back as I rolled him over. She acknowledged the dark blue, if not purple, color of his back, which indicates the body's pooling of blood due to gravity, denoting a good deal of time had passed after his demise. He was also stiff from rigor mortis, which also indicated a much longer time frame than the NA had stated.

I looked at the RN and asked, "How long do you think this gentleman has been dead?" She said, "Quite a while, I would think." I then began my rant, as I stared once again at the NA with an occasional glance at the RN. I said with a stern voice, "A Boy Scout with one hour of training would have been able to tell this man was dead and had been for a long time. But you (looking again at the NA) say you saw him take his last breath and started CPR. My God, how long have you been doing CPR, a couple of hours?" It obviously was a rhetorical question, and the sarcasm I believe is what took its toll. The NA began to cry and shouted, "I don't have to take this shit, I quit!" She turned around and walked off. I looked back at the RN supervisor and said, "Good, we have probably saved many lives here tonight."

Most nursing home residents will wait until the need is great prior to calling for a NA or RN. When they hit the buzzer, they usually truly require immediate assistance. I understand the nursing homes cannot have a one-to-one ratio of nursing staff to patients on their floors, but one-to-thirty or even one-to-twenty is unacceptable. True, I do not run a nursing home—never have, never will—but come on, there must be a better way.

This is one example of many, but the lack of quality care is the norm rather than the exception. We do not take particularly good care of our elderly and, horribly, that is a systemic problem. We all want to believe we are doing the right thing, and sometimes we have no other choice due to finances or the medical condition itself, I understand that. It just seems there could and should be a better way to deal with aging and the safekeeping of our parents once our ability to care for them has passed.

I would not be on the band wagon if I had only seen this type of thing happen once or twice in my career. I saw the extremely poor quality of care on a regular basis. I dare say, ask any field provider and see what they have to say about the subject. I am absolutely not by myself.

INCIDENT THIRTY-FOUR:
"HOLY ROLLER"

Going back in time again to when the EMS and fire departments were separate. The main times we interfaced were if someone was hurt in a fire or if we called for assistance with an automobile crash where someone was trapped.

Our EMS station had at one time been a small service station with two bays. The office was exceedingly small, and the back room was turned into a four-person bunk room. There were two stacked bunks that had been constructed by one of our paramedics. In the office, we had a desk that took up half of the room, small sofa and a TV up in the corner.

The city's first career EMS station, photographed in 1985.

At first, we worked eight-hour shifts, but soon thereafter we migrated to twelve hours per shift. Somehow that ended up morphing into ten-hour days and fourteen-hour nights, which yielded forty-eight-hour weeks. I do not remember how long it took, but we eventually went to twenty-four-hour shifts. One shift on, one shift off, one on, one off, one on, four off—that gave us all three shifts, or a seventy-two-hour work week. The catch was that we had to be at the station for twenty-four hours straight. The advantage for the employee was the four-day break. One could take off three consecutive shifts, and it yielded an entire week off. The bite was with EMS we were usually busy all night and those twenty-four-hour shifts took their toll.

There was a little church next to our station. The building had housed a laundromat, a pornographic bookstore, and a Chinese restaurant. It usually got loud on Sunday morning. The singing and the music poured out from the little cinderblock building. The minister and the people who ran the church were nice enough, but it was not my style of religion with all the yelling, guitars, banjoes, tambourines, and such. So, I pretty much kept my distance from the place.

One morning, Bill and I were sitting in the station, either watching TV or listening to another of Bill's exceptionally long stories. Bill was the captain of the volunteer crew that helped man the station. We got to know each other rather well, and he was most definitely a good old soul…for the most part.

Bill was married to Sarah, the first lieutenant of the crew. You have already heard about Sarah, and you will hear more later.

Bill and I heard someone yelling outside, and we walked out to investigate and saw dark smoke billowing from the front door and eaves of the little church building. We could hear people inside the building screaming for help. We told a man who was standing outside to call 9-1-1, and Bill and I went in through the front door. The smoke was very dark, but it had banked down only a couple of feet from the ceiling, which gave us good visibility and almost fresh air to breathe. We hurried to the back of the smoky room, and two ladies were huddled together crying for help. Bill took one and I the other, and we escorted them rapidly out of the burning structure.

Keep in mind, the fire station that responded to the 9-1-1 call was only a block away from the EMS station. We could see it from the church.

After we brought the two ladies out to safety, I asked one of them if there was anyone else in the building. She said she was not sure. I looked at Bill and told him to stay with the ladies and that I would run back in right quick and make sure there were no other people inside. Running into a burning building without proper equipment the first time was stupid. Going back in the second time was just plain dumb.

I had to duck down much further as I rapidly walked to the rear of the structure and yelled several times. I could not see anyone else, and no one answered my calls, so I turned to retreat to the front door. I made it about halfway back, but the smoke had banked much lower and I was not able to bend over enough to avoid taking it into my lungs. I dropped to my knees and tried to crawl out, but to my dismay, I did not make It. I was overcome by the smoke and passed out not far from the front door.

About that time, the engine company and an EMS crew arrived. Bill told them I was still inside. They immediately donned their gear and entered the structure to find me passed out on the floor. They dragged me out of the building and passed me off to the EMS crew waiting outside.

I do not remember the firefighters dragging me out. I do not fully recall the ride to the hospital. When my memory becomes much clearer is when the nurse stuck my wrist to access the artery for a carbon monoxide test. Damn if that didn't hurt! The EMS crew had me on high-flow O2 with a non-rebreather mask, they monitored my heart with an EKG, and they had started an IV, all en route to the ED. The treatment the crew had initiated was continued in the hospital, and they kept me overnight for observation.

By the way, surprise, I did not die that day, and I will be forever appreciative of the firefighters who pulled me out as quickly as they did.

Moral of this story: don't go into a burning building without proper gear, and for God's sake, do not be stupid enough to do it twice.

INCIDENT THIRTY-FIVE:
"PORN WALL"

Some days in the crazy world of fire-EMS, turn into exactly that, crazy. This incident occurred late one afternoon and extended into the evening. The call originally came from a person who thought they could smell natural gas near an apartment building. The building was occupied by thirty or so families. The response was first made by Engine-2, Ladder-2, Battalion Chief-2, Medic-2, and you guessed it, RS-1.

Battalion Chief-2 arrived with the other equipment from Station 2 and assumed command. The person who had called it in was still there and escorted several of our fire-EMS personnel to the place of interest. When they arrived at the C-D corner (If you were looking at the building from the street side, side A was dead ahead, side B was to the left, side C was in the rear, and side D was on the right.) the smell of gas was pervasive enough that the hazmat crew was immediately notified to respond.

Unfortunately, or fortunately, most of the hazmat crew was housed at Station 2, so all someone really had to do was go to the station and bring back a couple of apparatuses to the scene along with a few more people.

This task was carried out by the personnel from Station 5. So now we had Battalion Chief-2, Engine-2, Ladder-2, Medic-2, Engine-5, Hazmat, and RS-1.

The gas company was notified, and we started evacuating people from the apartments as well as the buildings on either side and to the rear. Both buildings on the left and right (Sides B and D) were businesses, and the building on side C was a private residence.

The gas company arrived soon after they were called and advised that they had a natural gas main break and that we needed to evacuate a larger number of buildings, increasing the perimeter exponentially.

Three businesses directly across the street were also designated as inside the perimeter and had to be cleared, as well.

This entire operation started reasonably small and rapidly grew to a large one. We had dealt with broken gas lines in the past, but this one seemed to take on a life of its own. Due to the large number of people who had to be evacuated, the police pitched in and at one time the reverse 9-1-1 system, which would notify large numbers of people by phone, was considered but ultimately not used.

We went from building to building advising the occupants that they were required to leave the premises immediately by order of the city fire-EMS and police due to a gas leak. This information was repeated numerous times by bullhorn, yelling, and simply talking face-to-face.

I'll bet you are wondering why this incident is named "Porn Wall" instead of something like, "Explosion in the Night" or "Street Sweep" or "Run for Your Life." Well, here we go:

In the process of evacuating the surrounding businesses, I ended up going into a "book and video" shop. I had heard about this shop, but I swear I had never previously been inside. I opened the door and walked in to find one man behind the counter. He was a thin, balding man with obviously dyed black hair, probably in his late fifties or so. I tried diligently to look him in the eyes as I delivered my announcement, but my eyes continuously wandered to the wall behind him. I am not exactly sure what they are all used for or for that matter why there were so many, but...the entire wall was covered with a vast variety of dildos. Yup...dildos. Big ones, small ones, pink ones, black ones, white ones—and if memory serves, even orange ones—and all in a multitude of lengths and widths.

I do remember asking the gentleman behind the counter, "How many people are here?" He stated, "We are full." I replied, "And that would be...?"

He followed with, "About twenty." My next question was "Well, where are they?" He said, "They're in the rooms."

I walked down a narrow hallway with sticky floors. I began knocking on doors and stating, "This building is being evacuated by the order of the city fire-EMS department due to a natural gas main break. Exit now through the front door!"

I continued to bang on the doors and repeated the comment many times. A few minutes passed, then men in all types of clothing slowly opened the doors and walked out. Guys with short pants, jeans, suits, and some still pulling their pants up. Yuck!

One man in a three-piece suit walked up to me and requested going out the back door. I did not let him. He shrugged and walked out the front door with his head hung low. No pun intended.

Now you know, the porn wall was long and wide. You just cannot make this shit up.

The gas company eventually turned the gas line off and made their repairs. The residents returned to their homes, and I am sure as the day is long—and wide—the porn wall lived on.

INCIDENT THIRTY-SIX:
"THERE GOES THE JUDGE"

I must admit, I have only had one of this type of EMS run in my lengthy career. I have appeared in court many times as a witness and have interacted with many bailiffs, sheriff's deputies, police officers, attorneys, and judges. This time it was a bit different to say the least, and my interaction started with a phone call from dispatch. Dispatch rarely called me on the phone to send me on an EMS run. It was not entirely unheard of, but rather rare.

The dispatcher told me I needed to go to the circuit courthouse and gave me the courtroom number, and that I was to see the bailiff prior to entering the courtroom. The dispatcher did not give me the nature of the call, nor did he say who I might be assisting. I was also advised to run silent and without lights. This clandestine meeting was starting to pique my curiosity, but being the public servant that I was, I responded as requested.

Upon my arrival to the courthouse, I was met by two sheriff's deputies and quickly escorted to the third floor where I was to speak with the bailiff.

The bailiff approached and began with, "I have no freakin' idea what the hell to do." OK, again, my degree of curiosity went through the roof. I asked, "And what the hell are we talking about?" He said, "You don't know? Well, the judge was hearing a case, and I noticed he seemed not to be paying attention to the attorneys when they were presenting their sides. I walked up to the judge and as I spoke to him, he fell backwards out of his chair and onto the floor. I could...you have to keep this under your hat...I could smell the strong odor of alcohol."

"Let me get this straight." I said, "You are telling me the judge is drunk as shit, and he is hearing cases?" The bailiff looked at me, shrugged his shoulders, and simply said, "Yes."

I then followed with, "What the hell do you expect me to do?" The bailiff said, "You're the EMS captain, the supervisor, right?" I nodded. He said, "I was hoping you might be able to get him to go to the hospital."

"Does he want to go?" I asked. "Well, not really," was the reply.

I told them that I would go into the courtroom and see what I found, and I needed at least one of them in there with me. The bailiff apparently had the best relationship with the judge, so he elected to accompany me. About the time I walked in, the judge once again had slumped out of his chair and onto the floor. I approached him, and as I did, I could swear—as a matter of fact, I do swear—I saw a slight seizure. I told the high officer of jurisprudence I was going to help him and that I needed to take his blood pressure along with the rest of his vital signs. The judge was rather blunt, I suppose, when behind the bench and that had not changed. He snapped "Get your fucking hands off me!" That of course made the interaction just a tad strained. I then advised him that he had possibly had a seizure or, for that matter, even a stroke. His expletives continued at an increased rate, and my responses up to that point had been what I would refer to as extremely professional. I could also smell the strong odor of alcohol.

I looked at the bailiff and then back at the judge. That is when I had an epiphany. I said, "Your Honor, you wish for me to leave you alone, correct?" The response was similar in nature to every other word that he had been uttering. I moved about ten feet away, and I said, "Then stand up and walk to me." He pushed up from the floor and made it back to his seat. As he attempted to stand, he fell forward, and I moved in to slow his descent. The bailiff and I both agreed that the judge had to go. I looked at him and asked him to smile, then grimace. After that I tried to get him to hold both arms out straight and he could not. I asked him who the president was; if memory serves, he came up with something like Lincoln or Taft. I asked him what the day of the week was, and he could not answer that simple question either.

I looked him dead in the eyes and said, "Your Honor, I deem you to be incompetent, and I am taking you to the hospital for evaluation of a possible stroke and/or seizure, if not alcohol toxicity." At that point, he shouted out a few more expletives, of which I am not sure I had ever heard before. The next comment he made was, "I am the fucking judge! You can't do this! I'll have your goddamned job!" My kindhearted response was, "Watch me."

During our conversation, which lasted about thirty minutes or so, I asked dispatch to have a medic unit respond and stand by with a stretcher. I called for the medics to come in, as well as a couple of the sheriff's deputies.

We carefully picked up the wayward judicial blob and placed him on the stretcher. He started spiting and trying to bite so I gave the order to restrain him, which they did.

He was placed in the back of the ambulance and transported to the hospital emergency department (ED). I called the ED communications officer and advised what we had and that the judge was extremely belligerent except during the times of near unconsciousness.

The judge was admitted and treated for acute alcohol toxicity. He also did have a couple of seizures. I felt bad about having to restrain him, but it was the only thing I could come up with at the time.

Not long after this occurrence, I heard that the good judge retired from the bench, and then a few years later he passed away.

I cannot help but think of all the defendants that went before him. To this day I wonder what happened to them and how many did or did not deserve what they received from that judge.

INCIDENT THIRTY-SEVEN:
"DOGGONE IT"

"Search and rescue" quite often turns rapidly into body recovery, and in this incident, in fact, it did. We were originally dispatched for a man who was being chased by the police who had jumped into the river that ran through the middle of our fair city. His attempted escape apparently had turned into a permanent solution for a temporary problem.

The area of the river he jumped into was about twenty feet deep and had a rapid current. The river ran through a park and under a couple of low-lying bridges, downstream from the jump-off location. The bridge had three large culverts and was in the portion of the river where we would usually end up finding bodies of unfortunate ones.

I was dispatched to meet up with the incident commander from the city police department. They had already pulled their command post trailer to an area near the river in a city park. The trailer was about thirty-five feet long and was extremely well-equipped. I climbed in to find Lieutenant Lewis sitting at a long desk decked out with satellite phones and banks of cell phones and a large bank of portable radios sitting in a bank of chargers on a wall, with extra batteries nearby. On a far wall there were several twelve-gauge shotguns and AR-15 rifles all locked into a gun rack.

The desk had a multitude of yellow legal pads and sharp pencils along with a couple of cans full of pens and different colored permanent markers. Lieutenant Lewis and I had worked together on a multitude of cases in the past and were familiar with each other's capabilities as well as strong points, thus the joint command.

A large map of the city and surrounding area was on the wall, and we began to mark off areas that had been searched. The police had been searching the riverbanks for several hours prior to my involvement, and the sun had only been up for about an hour when I arrived.

Approximately six hours had already passed since the jumper took the plunge. The police had devoted about twenty officers to the search, and my department was rapidly coming up with about fifteen men and women, as well as our swift-water rescue team.

I recommended we request assistance from the state police and a local medical helicopter service to assist in the search. If the body had made it past the culverts under the low bridge, then several miles of river would be available for the body to travel prior to going over a low water dam.

Lieutenant Lewis contacted the state police dispatcher and made the request, and I called the hospital dispatcher and requested their assistance.

The state police would be able to devote one Bell 206 Long Ranger to the cause for most of the day and the Bell 412 from the hospital would be with us so long as they did not receive a request for an emergency flight.

One helicopter was directed to the low water dam and to proceed north to the jump location and the other bird was directed to begin their search from the jump location and proceed south. They had several miles of river to search and having the eyes in the sky were most helpful at the very least.

We also had a couple of small boats at the command post and had them deployed with a police officer and a fire-EMS member. Their job was to continue searching the area near the jump location. They were both utilizing long poles, trying to search as much of the bottom of the river as possible. We had thought about divers, but the river was too muddy, and they would have had zero visibility. That was deemed too dangerous for the divers.

The search continued for the better part of the day, and it was getting dark. The eyes in the sky flew back to their respective helipads, the swift water rescue team packed up their equipment near the command post, and we called the search off for the night.

The following morning Lieutenant Lewis and I met up at the command post and started the process over again. The state police were able to devote the Bell 206 again, but the air ambulance was out on an emergency flight at the time.

We had been searching for about six more hours, and I contacted a gentleman who owned a couple of cadaver search dogs, and he agreed to join in on the search. He lived in another county but was only about an hour away. When he arrived, he asked for anything the dogs could use to obtain the subject's scent. The police had a shirt with the man's scent on it. The dogs sniffed and sniffed, and they got very excited about the search.

The man with the dogs requested a boat and an operator for the boat. They were supplied, and as the gentleman was about to get into the small vessel, I asked what he thought the chances were he could locate the body? He looked me dead in the eye and with an extremely serious look stated, "I'll have the body located within thirty minutes." I retorted, "Can I take that to the bank?" He simply stated, "Absolutely." I smiled and walked away. As I returned to the command post, the man was ushering his dogs into the boat.

After approximately twenty minutes, I walked back to where the boat had launched. The dogs suddenly both went to the port side of the boat and one of them stuck his nose into the water and began shaking his head back and forth violently. The proud owner of the dogs said, "The body is right here." I skeptically looked at him and advised our swift water team to join the man and his dogs and try searching with their long poles. They were in approximately twenty feet of water. They poked around in the area indicated by the dogs and, son-of-a-bitch, up popped the body of our runner/jumper.

The body was retrieved and had apparently been hung up on some structure on the bottom of the river. The medical examiner (ME)'s office was notified and responded to the scene in a nondescript white panel van.

In the meantime, the police death scene investigators took some photos, as did the ME's office death investigator. The body was tagged and placed into a black body bag. The ME's investigator loaded the body into the van and departed the scene. In the meantime, the state police dispatcher was notified that the body had been located and that we appreciated their assistance. The rest of the search teams had also been notified and had returned to the command post. After everyone was thanked for their participation and dismissed, the command post was shut down and hooked back up to a truck and towed back to the police impound lot.

I spoke with the owner/trainer of the cadaver dogs a few days later and told him he had made me a believer and that I would be calling him again in the future. He advised me that the dogs worked better after the body had been submerged for a few days due to the gases let off by the decaying body. The gases floated to the surface and that was what the dogs had keyed on. They certainly did a remarkable job and saved the city a lot of time and effort trying to locate that poor lost soul.

INCIDENT THIRTY-EIGHT:
"EXPLOSION"

Back in the day, most of the fire-EMS personnel worked twenty-four-hour shifts. This gave each of us the opportunity to supplement our salary, which was at that time minimal. Most of us had two, three, and sometimes four jobs at one time. A lot of the firefighters elected to do things like roofing, cleaning windows, driving propane delivery trucks, and other assortments of menial or other jobs they could fit into their regular schedule. Normally, working as a firefighter gave that individual the opportunity to work two full-time jobs. They knew the chances were that they would be able to get enough sleep to go directly from one job to the other.

When the merger occurred and the firefighters had to start actively running EMS calls, their sleep habits had to change. Most of the full-time second jobs went by the wayside, and part-time jobs became much more popular.

On the EMS side, personnel knew they would be active most, if not all, of the shift, and other jobs had to fit into a busy schedule. Sleep was as important as a second job. Sleep deprivation was something we lived with from day to day. At the same time, we also had to be able to pay the bills— therefore, we all took second jobs. Some of us worked multiple side jobs that had very flexible schedules.

My choice for a "primary" second job was that of a flight medic with the local trauma center. When I first hired on, I had only been working as a paramedic on the streets for about two years. One of our part-time medics happened to be the flight team coordinator for the program.

We were assigned to the same shift and got to know each other fairly well. One afternoon we were sitting around the station, and he asked me if I had ever thought of becoming a flight medic. I quickly answered negatively. The fact that a multitude of medical helicopters had crashed over the past year was the cause of some of my hesitancy. At the same time, I certainly could use the additional income. My wife was a schoolteacher, and I a fledgling paramedic. Neither job produced a plethora of financial gain, so I decided to investigate the possibility.

I went to the headquarters for the flight service and spoke with a couple of the pilots and paramedics who had been flying for several years. At that point in time, they had just started employing flight nurses. The helicopter they were using was a Bell 206 Jet Ranger and was not capable of carrying more than the pilot, the paramedic, and the patient. When the hospital purchased a Bell 222A, the capability grew exponentially. We could carry two patients with two attendants and the pilot. The only problem occurred when it was hot outside. The bird could only carry so much weight.

I remember the pilot pulling up slowly from the helipad, backing up just to the edge of the pad, and then trying to get a little run-and-go. Sometimes this would be repeated several times before the bird launched upward.

The Federal Aviation Administration (FAA) apparently figured out what was causing most of the crashes of medical helicopters. Pilot fatigue was labeled as the main problem, and the fix was to hire a fourth pilot onto the crew. Three pilots were trying to keep up with multiple shifts of nurses and paramedics. They were just overworked. The fourth pilot made a world of difference. We would still hear of the occasional crash around the country but not at the same frequency and not all due to the fatigue of the pilot.

OK, once again, I have found myself off topic a bit. The fact that I worked at both places, however, is pertinent to the storyline.

The call originally came in as a fire in a backyard work shed. It was also stated that a subject was on the scene with severe burns. Engine-11 (E-11), Medic-1 (M-1), and Rescue Supervisor-1 (RS-1) were dispatched, and we all

RED LIGHTS & BEYOND

kicked into gear and responded. We all arrived about the same time, and the captain on E-11 assumed command and made quick work of the shed. The patient had been inside the shed when gasoline fumes apparently filled the space, and a spark from whatever ignited the "bomb." This poor guy had flash burns all over his body. His clothes had been mostly burned off, and his skin was dripping from his arms and legs. His face was void of facial hair as was most of his head. He was alert and oriented, which was a little strange and at the same time sad. I knew I was dealing with a walking, talking dead guy.

We put out the fire from the clothing that was still hanging onto his body and placed him on the stretcher and put him into the ambulance. We applied dry burn sheets and put on O2 with a non-rebreather mask. As the other paramedic tried to initiate a couple of large-bore IV lines, I advised the driver to go—fast. I expected our patient to go unconscious during the transport, but he did not, so I was unable to intubate. We could just barely get a decent EKG strip due to the dripping skin.

Both of us were extremely busy in the back of M-1. I called the hospital Med-Com and gave my report: "We have a burn patient with approximately ninety-five percent of the body with second- and third-degree burns. The patient was in an enclosed area during a gasoline fume explosion." I continued, "The patient is still alert and oriented with a respiratory rate of forty and shallow. Pulse is one hundred-twenty beats per minute and showing sinus tach on the EKG. An estimated systolic pressure of sixty due to the carotid pulse being present with absent radial pulses. Two large-bore IV lines of saline, sixteen gauge in the left AC (inside bend of the elbow) and a fourteen gauge in his right AC are both running wide open along with high-flow O2 via non-rebreather. We have an ETA of five minutes."

222

We got him to the trauma center technically alive, and as we drove back to the scene to pick up my vehicle, we were not betting he would survive the night if that.

The following day, I was signed up for an early shift at the same trauma center's air ambulance service. About the time I walked in, the "Red" phone rang out with a flight request from our hospital to the nearest burn center.

I always hated flying burn patients because it was exceedingly difficult to get the odor of burned flesh and hair out of my nostrils. It lingered for days.

The flight nurse and I went to the hospital to make their patient ours and to make ready for the flight. I looked at the now-unconscious intubated patient still with the two lines started in the field and bandages all over his body.

I found it hard to believe that he was still alive—plus, the fact that now I had to fly him to another institution that was about an hour and a half away by air. We prepped the patient by switching over his IV lines to our pumps, and I took over the airway by bagging him until we could set him up on our ventilator.

As we loaded him onto our stretcher, I looked at the intensive care unit nurse who had been working with the patient, and we both kind of just shook our heads, knowing full well the injuries he had sustained were not compatible with survival.

We loaded our patient into the helicopter and set him up on the onboard vent. This allowed both of us, his attendants, to work with medication administrations, monitor his vitals, communicate by radio with the receiving facility, and fill out paperwork.

The smell of burned flesh permeated the air inside the helicopter, to the point of near nausea. The flight was pretty much uneventful, and we spoke with the receiving facility during the flight via their Med-Com channel. They had a stretcher waiting on the helipad, and the transfer was smooth. We officially turned the patient over to the burn center personnel in their burn unit and removed our IV pumps. Before we left the unit, I spoke with the nurse about to take charge of this patient and advised him of the extent of the burns. He said it would be a miracle if the patient lasted the night. I concurred and walked away. We arrived back at the helipad, climbed back into the Bell 412SP, buckled up our four-point restraints, plugged into the flight com, and as I gazed at the pilot, giving him a thumbs-up for takeoff, without any spoken words, both of us shook our heads.

After a few minutes in the air the silence was broken as we discussed the inevitable outcome of our burn patient. We had all seen similar situations in the past and were not surprised when we heard that the patient died the next day. The surprise was that he made it out of that shed alive and lived to make the trip to the burn center.

INCIDENT THIRTY-NINE:
"NAILED IT"

It had been an average day on the job. Running with the city fire-EMS Department always meant a busy day but not always dramatic, from my perspective—which I might say is a little bit strange.

The weather report had come in for some occasional thunderstorms in the mid-to-late afternoon. I had noticed some rather dark clouds rolling in, but it really did not concern me at the time.

A large group of workers were in the process of setting up several large tents on city property in anticipation of a large event. I honestly don't remember what the event was going to be. I just vividly remember the call coming in on the radio.

The dispatcher spoke up, "Engine-8, Medic-8, Engine-5, Medic-1, Rescue Supervisor-1, Battalion Chief-1, respond to 202 River Drive to the city park; large tree fell onto several workers; subjects trapped." All of us marked up and en route on the radio.

I arrived on scene first and knowing BC-1 was almost there, I deferred from taking command and started to try and triage patients, if needed. A large sycamore tree that was completely full of bright green leaves had apparently been blown over while the folks on the ground were trying to put up a forty-foot-long tent. The storm blew up and produced some rather impressive straight-line winds. By the time we arrived, the weather had completely changed over to mostly cloudy, but most of us had seen the dark ominous clouds just a bit earlier.

I marked on scene, "RS-1 on scene at 202 River Drive, with a large tree that has fallen onto two subjects I am told. I will be out investigating." As soon as I arrived, a man came over to my vehicle and advised there were two people under the tree. I found out later the tree had hit three others, but they were all relatively unhurt.

I approached the tree, and I could hear a man calling for help. As I worked my way through the tree's large branches, I heard the other units arriving on my radio. I found my way to the man, and he screamed, "She's over there! I'm OK, just trapped! I think she is hurt!" I acknowledged and wrapped some yellow triage tape high on one of the branches. I called BC-1, who had established command: "Command, RS-1." BC-1 responded, "Command, go ahead RS-1." I continued, as I found the other victim, "Command, I need a Lifepak 10 brought to me, and we will need a couple of chain saws for extrication. I marked patient number one's location with yellow triage tape. He appears to be trapped but not seriously injured. I just located number two and this one will probably be a DOA. I'll confirm with the Lifepak monitor." His response was, "OK."

When I walked up to the young lady, I could see her skin color was blue, and I was able to move a branch or two to gain slight access to her back and the back of her neck. I checked for a pulse and there was none. The tree had driven the poor soul into the ground. She was bent over with a large tree branch on her back with extraordinarily little space between the branch and the ground.

One of the firefighters brought the Lifepak to me, and I did a quick look with the paddles to confirm what I already knew. As I worked with the young lady, others were working on trying to get to the man out. In the meantime, two more people showed up with minor scratches and bruises.

All in all, we had one unfortunate young lady along with two other minor injuries, plus one extremely lucky guy. The man who was trapped was just that. Trapped but no injuries, not even a scratch, go figure.

INCIDENT FORTY:
"TOO HOT TO HANDLE"

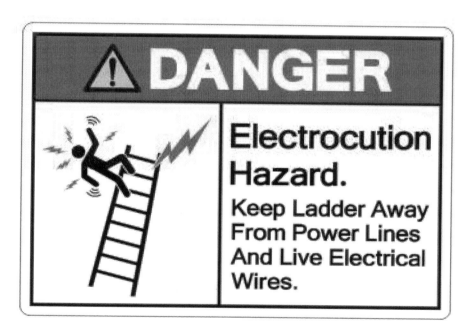

Another call rang out at the station: Engine-9 (consisting of a fire captain, a fire lieutenant, and two firefighters), Medic-4 (with one career paramedic and one volunteer EMT), and Rescue Supervisor-1 (, as you have figured by now, was me). The dispatcher continued, "Respond to a possible electrocution, 5747 Skylark Avenue, go to the back of the building." And she, as always, gave the time of day and then repeated everything one more time. Our dispatchers over time got to know most of us very well. We depended on their professionalism as they did ours.

Apparently, a young man had been working on a gutter and his ladder contacted an overhead power line. He was well-grounded with the ladder sitting on a wet metal plate and no rubber or plastic on the feet of the ladder. The occupants of the building came outside when the power went off and they heard a loud bang, which was probably one of the large breakers on the pole exploding. One of the ladies looked around the side of the building and found our patient. She had been the one to call 9-1-1.

I later told her that was an astute observation, recognizing a possible electrocution. She stated that she had basically just put two-and-two together.

The engine company and I arrived at the same time and advised dispatch we were on the scene. I exited my vehicle as the firefighters exited theirs. As we walked around the side of the building, we could see two people standing and one man supine on a large metal plate. There was a ladder beside them, on the ground. The crew from Engine 9, recognizing the situation, began CPR on the patient. I began to try and get a history of what had just occurred as Medic-4 was close behind. I was speaking with the bystanders as I obtained my Lifepak 5 to perform a quick look, as I had before, a thousand times it seemed.

I spread a little gel onto the paddle and rubbed them together. I placed the paddles on the victim's chest to find "fine V-Fib" (fine ventricular fibrillation). His heart was trembling from electrical activity all over the ventricles. I charged the paddles to prepare to shock the patient. Then I realized we were all standing on a wet metal plate, so I decided to move the patient off the plate and onto the ground. I am not sure if discharging the paddles would have fried all of us, but I am glad we did not find out the hard way.

At any rate, I shocked the patient and then noted "coarse V-Fib" on the scope. I said, "Clear, CLEAR" as I re-armed the paddles, and after a third "CLEAR" I shocked him again. I had cured him of the coarse V-fib; now he was in "asystole"— that's the one you see on TV, the straight line, when everyone walks away and the team leader says, "Good job. Time of death 17:46." About that time, Medic-4 arrived, and we continued to work on the patient as diligently as we possibly could. This guy was about twenty-five years old, and what a waste if he were to die.

The medic from Medic-4 had attempted to intubate the patient several times but was unable to pry his jaws apart due to "trismus," which was caused by the initial electrical shock and contraction of his jaw muscles. She yelled for me to assist with airway management. With the young man still in cardiac arrest now for almost too long, I decided to go with transtracheal jet insufflation (TTJI). Well, this was to be the first time anyone, at least in this state, had attempted this medical maneuver in the field. We had all been taught how to do it by sticking the necks of dead dogs. I kept everything I needed in a kit. That way I could connect to oxygen supply lines in most medical vehicles as well as institutions. Plus, if necessary, it was also portable with an O2 tank in tow.

To continue: I pierced the patient's neck at the cricothyroid membrane, near the base of the Adam's Apple, with a twelve-gauge three-inch angiocath and advanced it and then the catheter into his trachea, just below the vocal cords. I then attached the line from the cath to the valve, which allowed me to ventilate the poor soul. Here is a photo of the original TTJI demand valve. I made this "medical device" from a common service station air gun. I sanded the metal tip down to fit the butt end of an angiocath. All I had to do for setup was to attach my gun to the end of an O2 hose line and I was ready to stick the patient's neck. One of my favorite medical directors, who was also a superb ER physician, made one for himself. We both used them until the new medical director emphatically said "NO!" Non-medically approved devices would not be used." We complied and then found a medically approved valve on the market and bought one for each medic unit and RS-1. I bought one for myself.

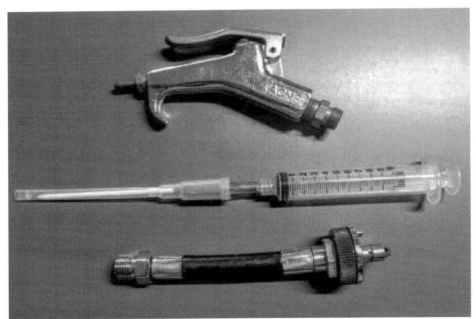

My homemade transtracheal jet insufflation demand valve.

And yes, the handle really does say ACME, but I swear I did not steal it from Wile E. Coyote. In the photo, one also will notice the twelve-gauge three-inch angiocath attached to a ten-cc syringe. The adapter at the bottom of the photo would enable me to attach the device to a medical vehicle's onboard O2, as well as most hospital in-house oxygen supplies.

Back to our unfortunate young man. As I stated earlier, this would be the initial attempt of a TTJI, and I was damned nervous. I had stuck the dogs many times, and I taught other medics and even doctors and nurses how to perform the procedure. But this time it was in the field on a dying human.

I continued to ventilate our patient but, he was unable to cooperate. The trace on the EKG continued to look extremely poor. Several drugs were administered, and I think he was shocked once again on the scene. We packaged him as we continued working the code. We placed him in the ambulance as I walked in backwards at the head of the stretcher and continued to ventilate the patient. That would be my sole job from that time until he was turned over to the hospital staff.

Upon arrival to the hospital ER, one of the nurses approached as if we were criminals. She snapped, "YOU cannot do that! Only a doctor can do that!" I just looked at her and said, "Well, apparently, we can. Please just take the turnover and take care of your patient." It looked like she did not get the memo about our field protocols. As the EMS supervisor, I was approved for the procedure without having to make a request from the hospital. Unfortunately, this young man did not survive, but a lot was learned from this event, and the lessons helped others successfully.

INCIDENT FORTY-ONE:
"NO HOSPITAL, NO DOC"

I am going to call our next patient Albert. Albert was twenty-one years old when we first met. I was the paramedic responding to a call for seizures. Keep in mind this was the time when there would be only one career medic and a volunteer EMT at the wheel of the medic unit.

Sarah, my aforementioned sidekick, and I arrived to find a young adult male supine on the floor during a grand mal seizure. He was flailing and his body was jumping as if struck with a defib paddle. He had already bloodied the back of his head and urinated on himself. Most seizures end after a short time. But some are longer than others, and then you have legitimate cases of "status epilepticus," which is just a seizure that will not stop and requires emergency care. This incident turned out to be the latter.

The airway is always a major concern with status epilepticus. His mother was able to give us a medical history that he had been plagued with seizures all his life, but recently they were lasting longer and longer. This one had already been going for fifteen to twenty minutes prior to her calling 9-1-1.

I took control of his airway and tried to ventilate with a bag-valve mask. I ended up strapping a non-rebreather on him. I held down his arm enough to get an IV started and called in to the hospital requesting orders for Valium, which was the only anti-convulsant we carried.

The fact I had to request orders for Valium should alone place a date on this incident. I ended up giving him ten milligrams of Valium, and it did not even touch him. If memory serves, they gave orders for an additional five milligrams and then I started en route to the hospital. It was all I could do to keep his airway open. I had hoped we could break the seizure and then he would be much easier to handle. As it was, Sarah was driving, and I was dealing with Albert in the back of the unit by myself.

We got to the hospital and a respiratory tech and a nurse from the emergency room hopped into the back of the unit, and the help was greatly appreciated. As soon as they climbed in, the nurse said, "Well Albert, fancy meeting you here." I said, "You know him?" She replied, "If I had a nickel for every time he has been by to visit."

Albert was removed from the ambulance, and as we made it into the trauma room, the nurse said, "It's Albert." Most of the people disappeared, back to whatever they were doing prior to finding out it was Albert. One nurse drew up a dose of phenobarbital. She took the IV line in one hand and the dose of phenobarbital in the other. Just a few minutes after the IV push, Albert stopped his seizure activity.

The valium didn't seem to work at all, but the phenobarbital worked like a charm. When Albert awoke from his fog, he was rather short with everyone. He did not appear to appreciate the fact that his life was just saved by the folks hanging out at his bedside.

A few days later, Albert's mother called 9-1-1 again for another seizure that would not stop. She called again and again and again.

The next time I had an encounter with Albert, on our arrival he was very cyanotic (blue skin color), which told us he was already in dire straits, and we needed to act quickly. I broke out my intubation equipment and Sarah set up for an IV line and applied the three-lead EKG pads. Albert's respirations were sixty and extremely shallow. He really was not moving very much air at all. I started by putting a nasal airway in and bagging him with 100 percent O2. The status seizure continued, and his heart rate was through the roof. I needed to get some O2 into his lungs and fast. I tried to hyperventilate him, but the air was just not making it to where it needed to go. The bag felt hard as a rock. This young man was dying right in front of me in the next few minutes if I could not access his lungs. His mouth was shut tight, and it took a bit to get the blade of the laryngoscope between his lips. He was suffering from hypoxia, which is the reduction or lack of oxygen exchange in the lungs. The seizure plus the hypoxia caused a reaction called trismus, which causes the jaws to clinch. I simply was unable to separate his upper jaw from his lower. His condition continued to go on and on, which exacerbated the situation exponentially.

The color of his skin was so cyanotic he looked like a damn Smurf. My only realistic choice of treatment was to do a needle trach. I unrolled my TTJI equipment. I proceeded with the procedure mentioned earlier. I could not stop the seizure, but I could help him breathe.

We loaded him into the medic unit, and off we went once again to the same ER and to the same reception. They would say something like, "No rush, it's just good ole Albert." They knew a good bolus of phenobarbital would do the trick.

I lost count how many times we responded to that same little house. I would venture it was a hundred or so. I know that does not sound possible, but it is pretty accurate. I am not saying that Albert didn't get the best possible treatment, because he absolutely did. It was just with the frequent repetition, and the fact he refused to take his medication on a regular basis.

I responded to Albert's house one afternoon, and the medic unit beat me there. They were working on Albert and trying to maintain a good airway with high-flow O2 and get an IV in him for med administration. I unbuttoned his shirt so I could pop an EKG monitor on him to find his chest marked very clearly with red lipstick "NO HOSP NO DOC." I just looked at it and went on as usual. If I could get to him in time, I could usually maintain his airway and supply O2 without advanced airways. Other times, it was either an endotracheal intubation or a TTJI. This time, I took him into the ER with a basic airway and bagging him. The ER doc decided to intubate Albert, and he was having a lot of difficulty visualizing his vocal cords. The doctor pulled back just a bit too far and I saw Albert's two front teeth crumble.

One day, Albert's mother called 9-1-1 again and the crew responded, knowing what they were going to encounter. They unfortunately were surprised this time. Albert was in full cardiac arrest, so they called a "code blue" on the radio, and assistance arrived via fire truck. They worked on Albert for quite some time to no avail. I can see his face and the writing on his chest to this day. He finally got the relief from his personal burden for which he had been clamoring. That last time, he got his last wish.

NO HOSP NO DOC

After about thirty minutes of trying to revive him, the medics pronounced Albert dead at his mother's home with her looking on.

INCIDENT FORTY-TWO:
"IN THE DITCH"

Long, rainy nights normally prevented our air ambulance service from flying, but sometimes the weather would clear just in the nick of time and make us available once again.

I have no idea where they were going or, for that matter, why they were out in their late-model sedan tooling down the road. What I do know is that the car exited the interstate highway onto the right shoulder and rolled at least once, ejecting two of the occupants.

Lynne and I were on duty with the local level one trauma center's emergency air ambulance service. We had one of the program's top pilots working with us that night by the name of Sam.

Sam had flown a Cobra hot and heavy in Vietnam and was one of the most, if not the most, accomplished helicopter pilots I have even known. If he took a flight after looking at the weather, I always felt comfortable climbing in the ole bird because I knew Sam would get us there and back safely, no questions asked.

Sometimes we would go an entire shift without a flight, and then, on the other hand, we could end up rather busy. This shift started off slowly, and then all the sudden the "hot line" to the hospital's Med-Com rang. Lynne picked it up and listened. We were being requested by a rural rescue squad that was on the scene of a vehicle crash on the nearby interstate highway. The car had run off the road and flipped an unknown number of times. The driver was thrown out, as was an eighteen-month-old baby. The mother was originally found in the front passenger seat with her seatbelt on.

Sam immediately looked up the location and did a quick check of the weather. There would sometimes be weather conditions that would preclude us from flying, and the pilot obviously was the one with the final say. This flight was a go. We all walked out to the massive Bell 412SP. Sitting still, she was a beautiful piece of equipment that was all put together to save lives. Sam climbed into the pilot's seat and started going over his preflight checklist. Lynne climbed in through the sliding side door and began to make ready for one or more patients.

While Sam and Lynne had their routine to go through, I walked over and rolled the APU to the front of the bird. I opened the small door on the nose of the machine and plugged it into the receiver. Then I waited for Sam to give me the signal to unplug.

In the early days with the Bell 222A, we used the same process, but we did not have the same degree of hearing protection. When I started with the hospital, we had little yellow earplugs attached to a cord to reduce the noise. By the time I left the service, we were wearing helmets that had hearing protection built in. They also had full communication capability with the pilot during startup via a plug-in for the onboard.com.

The pilot looked at me and gave a thumbs-up along with a short communication over the com. I disconnected the APU and rolled in back to the side of the helipad. I then walked over to the front left seat, or the co-pilots seat. This clearly did not make me a co-pilot; I was just occupying the space. With all three of us belted into our four-point harnesses, Sam called the hospital dispatcher and advised of our imminent departure. As the bird departed from the large square concrete pad, we vibrated a bit, and I remember hearing and literally feeling the power of that massive machine. Sam called the local airport tower and advised we were a "Lifeguard" mission, as well as our present location and destination. We rose from the little piece of concrete, which was shrinking rapidly. We flew just above several power lines and then rose rather rapidly. We had to stay above the buildings as well as the mountains that were nearby.

Speaking of mountains, it was dark, and we used the roads to keep us flying in a safe direction. As we rose a bit more, we could clearly see the familiar roads and use them to make our way out of town. The moon was shining enough to allow us to make out the tops of the mountains, and it was nice to have a friendly moon on this occasion.

While we were zipping across the city and off to the nearby county where the crash had occurred, I contacted the fire officer on the ground who oversaw the landing zone (LZ). I advised of our ETA and asked if he had any information about the subjects in question. He responded affirmatively and said, "The father is dead under the car, the mother is in bad shape but alive for the moment, and the baby was found face down in the water on the side of the road." They were working on the baby and the mother. It certainly sounded urgent, and it was.

The LZ, we were told, was set up in the middle of the interstate highway. As we came closer, the flashing red and blue lights of emergency vehicles became apparent, penetrating the darkness of the night for a great distance. We could see a long line of cars and trucks on the north and south sides of the interstate. Then the crash scene itself came into view, as did the LZ. Sam made his usual perfect approach to the LZ, as they had stated, in the middle of the interstate.

We set down, and Lynne and I both climbed out of the bird that was still moving every piece of loose dirt and sand it could find with the sixty-mile-per-hour downdraft from its rotors. We had all our equipment tied down to the stretcher, and we each took one end and carried it to the scene. I walked up to an EMT and asked who was in charge. He said, "The police, I guess." That wasn't exactly my intent, so I went to another EMT, and he apparently was the one in the know. He stated that a Good Samaritan had stopped at the scene and apparently had witnessed the crash. He had removed the baby from

244

the muddy pool of water, begun CPR, and resuscitated the infant. When we arrived, the baby appeared to be doing OK, but after that much trauma, one never knows.

The EMTs seemed to be doing fine with the baby. They were trying to keep him warm, and they had O2 running. The baby was moving about and was in no apparent respiratory difficulty. The mother, however, was a different ball game altogether. There is a term we would sometimes use when a patient was royally messed up: "fubar." If someone was "fubared," they were also known to be in "deep shit." This lady was both. She was the most critical, and we had a Basic Life Support (BLS) unit on scene to take the baby in, so we elected to medevac the mother. I intubated the mother as Lynne started a couple of large-bore IV lines. The EKG was showing atrial tach at a high rate, and her blood pressure was about eighty systolic.

As we were about to load her onto our stretcher for her flight back to the trauma center, she coded. Damn it, she went into cardiac arrest. I looked at Lynne and we both at the same time said, "Let's take the baby." I started unplugging the EKG and told the EMTs to go ahead and work her as a BLS code blue until either they got to the ER or the doctor on the Med-Com radio told them to stop. We switched the EKG over to the eighteen-month-old baby girl and assisted her with occasional puffs from the bag-valve mask. She was too alert to intubate, and her skin color looked good. She did have a bad raspy cough, but at least she was coughing. She had a considerable amount of bruising on her back and abdomen, which was also of concern. I stayed with the airway and monitored her heart rate. We were unable to obtain a blood pressure (BP), but she had radial pulses, which gave us an indication of a good BP. Lynne started an IV for fluid and a medication route if needed. We kept her warm and delivered her to the hospital still in the same shape as she was when we took off from the interstate just a few minutes prior.

The BLS crew with the mother arrived about forty-five minutes after we did, and the Med-Com doctor had called off the BLS code on the mother shortly after they left the scene.

Triage is sometimes difficult to follow through with. This time, however, it seemed a no-brainer. Dad was DRT (Dead Right There), mom lost her shot for a helicopter ride when she coded, and the baby…

Well, I would love to report that the baby survived and grew up to be a happy young lady. Unfortunately, I cannot. The baby girl died two weeks later from internal injury and chemical pneumonia from the inhalation of muddy water from the side of the road.

We were called to help, and we did the very best we could and made the decisions according to the book. I think about that call occasionally, and second guess on occasion. I don't know what else we could have done to avoid the loss of an entire family. Sometimes the best one can do just isn't fucking enough.

INCIDENT FORTY-THREE:
"ONE MORE SUICIDE, BY THE BOOK"

⚠ WARNING:
PLASTIC BAGS CAN BE DANGEROUS.
TO AVIOD DANGER OF SUFFOCATION
KEEP THIS BAG AWAY FROM BABIES
AND CHILDREN.

And dumb asses

There was a book, and I suppose it is still out there somewhere, on how to kill yourself. One of the options that was mentioned was capping everything off with a plastic bag. I had never encountered that method until this day.

We were called out to assist the police, who were already out on a wellbeing check. The caller said he had not been able to get in touch with his father for a couple of days, so he finally alerted the local police department and that put everything else into motion.

The police pulled up to the house and knocked on the door to no avail. They went through the normal progression of events. They tried to investigate by looking in the windows but couldn't see anything.

Generally, they don't like breaking into someone's home, and quite frankly, that can be extremely dangerous. They had refrained from doing any damage to the house, but their purpose there was to find out if the man was home or if something unfortunate had occurred.

Upon arrival of the EMS unit and myself, they stated they had checked all the doors and windows. Everything was locked solid, and the only way they could see to gain entry was to either break down a door or break a window. The thing you see on TV when the police break down a door by kicking it in with their foot—well, the only thing that gets damaged when they try that is their foot or their leg. Smart officers and fire/EMS folks break the smallest piece of glass necessary to gain entry. This may be beside a door or a window. Generally, the least damage we had to make, the better.

Many times, I had broken into a house to find no one home. I always made sure the family member requesting the wellbeing check was A-OK with whatever destruction was about to take place.

This time was no different. The police officer in charge and I concluded it was an appropriate decision to gain entry to the house. I carried a Halligan bar in my vehicle for just this purpose. The Halligan bar is a firefighting tool that is wonderful for prying a door jamb apart and opening the door, normally with minimal damage.

We popped the door open, and as soon as the air from the inside of the house tickled our olfactory senses, we all knew this was going to go south rapidly. Usually, we could get a rookie police officer to go in first. It was always fun to watch his or her face as the aroma got embedded in their nostrils. A lot of the experienced officers carried a cigar just for these moments. The cigar dampened the odor that was penetrating their sinus cavities. Most of us, the older and more experienced fire/EMS folks, got used to the smell of decaying flesh. Decomposition of the body is just that, and it has a very distinctive smell. Unpleasant as it is, it can become incidental. With some, however, it never seemed to get easier.

We entered the house and there were police officers with us as we walked carefully into the death scene. We searched several rooms until we made it to the dining room, which was a formal dining area and mostly closed off from all the other rooms. The subject was lying on the floor. He was dressed as if just about to go somewhere, and he had placed a plastic sheet under where his body would most likely come to rest. On the dining room table, we found a pill bottle of Vicodin and a glass, apparently of vodka. The pill bottle was empty and had a count of thirty listed. It had been filled ten days prior. I guess the pills were just to get him started, and the pièce de résistance was the clear plastic bag covering his head. It was closed by a couple of rubber bands. It looked as though he may have had second thoughts. His right hand was up around his neck and looked as if he had tried to remove the bag, or at least thought about it. Too little, too late. This also happened to be one of those situations that one cannot unsee. To this day, I can see in my mind's eye the plastic bag sucked into his mouth and nose. His last breaths did not appear to be as calm and soothing as he had anticipated. He had struggled at the end.

This had just become a police and medical examiner's scene and not an EMS scene. The man had obviously been involved in his last bit of glory a few days back.

I could go on and describe what a body looks like after the decomp processes has advanced. I'll spare you that, at least for now—no promises for later.

After obtaining as much information on the decedent as I could, I documented everything we had done, and when I returned to the station, I promptly wrote out my little dissertation on an EMS run report. On situations that were a bit out of the norm, I usually was much more thorough and would occasionally include an extra page or two of explanation just in case it ended up in court. That way I would have everything I needed to remind me of the call, documented. Judges really hate it when someone gets on the stand and has no clue what they are talking about. Plus, the opposing attorney will cut you to pieces if they find you guessing or making conjecture. As Joe Friday always said, "Just the facts."

INCIDENT FORTY-FOUR:
"MIRACLE DRUGS"

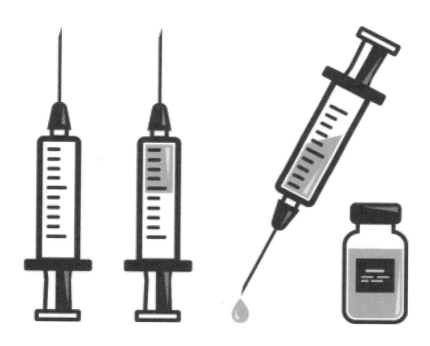

Originally, the call came in as a man unresponsive. The normal complement of equipment responded to the scene, including Medic-1 with two paramedics and Engine-9 with the engine captain, the lieutenant/operator, one FF/paramedic, and one FF/EMT. The engine company arrived first and saw a man flat on his back on the sidewalk. There were several people crowded around the subject, who was apparently unconscious. The FF/paramedic who was on board the engine quickly assessed the situation and radioed back to the responding medic unit that they had a man unresponsive and not breathing but with a weak pulse.

The medic unit was almost there, and upon hearing that they had a subject unresponsive not breathing, RS-1 was also dispatched. I then appropriately marked en route.

I was not very far from the scene and arrived at the same time Medic-1 marked on scene. The FF/EMT had already put in place an oral-pharyngeal airway and started ventilating their patient, and the FF/medic was in the process of applying EKG pads in case a defibrillation was appropriate and for continued monitoring of the heart. The two medics from Medic-1 joined in the fun and helped the attendants already working on the patient.

Upon my arrival, I walked over to several of the bystanders and asked if anyone knew the young man on the sidewalk. A couple of them had very concerned looks on their faces, and it was obvious to me that they did know the man. I asked again and made it clear that information from them to me was probably confidential. Yes, I said "probably."

I said, "If you know he has used any kind of drugs or if he has any known medical problems, you damn well better speak up or your friend is likely to die here, right in front of you!" One of the bystanders stated he, in fact, knew the patient and said, "He had been smoking pot and may have shot up some other shit." That was enough to get the unconscious young man a hit of Narcan. Narcan is, as you have probably heard in the news at some point, a medication that counteracts or reverses the effects of an opioid overdose. It is one of those things that defies reason. The patient could be on death's door, and after he gets a dose of Narcan, within a very short time, the patient wakes up and wants to know what the hell is going on. We found over time that if you woke up the person too much, too fast before you got to the hospital, the patient was likely to refuse transport. We had had at least one I know of who jumped out of the back of the ambulance as it was slowly rolling down the road. Our current patient really needed to go to the hospital at that point because the Narcan would eventually wear off and he very well might need additional doses.

We had another call not long after the opioid OD, and the call was dispatched pretty much the same way. This time it was Medic-8 and Engine-8. They didn't have very far to travel to the scene, and I simply stood pat where I was and just listened on the radio.

Many times, the medics would get on scene and recognize the patient or rapidly assess the situation and disregard RS-1. That is exactly what happened with this call. I found out later that the subject that was down on the street was a known brittle diabetic. Those medics had probably run twenty calls on that same person. They gave him some O2, pricked his finger to verify his blood sugar level, started an IV line of normal saline, and administered a bolus from a fifty-cc prefilled syringe, containing twenty-five grams of dextrose in water (D50).

This also happens to be one of the true medical miracles. Within moments of the D50 hitting the blood stream, the patient normally awakens to wonder why all these strange-ass people are around and WTF are these tubes. Face it, the brain needs sugar.

I had seen that rapid reaction so many times it almost became a game. We would administer D50, count to ten, and say good morning. Sometimes they would wake up before we could even get all the fifty-cc bolus into the bloodstream. Then again, sometimes it took a second bolus of twenty-five grams to wake them up. It was always convenient when the diabetic patients wore an ID tag stating their medical problem. Some had ID cards in their billfold or purse. Medic Alert Tags are truly wonderful little things. They really do save lives.

Another one of the "miracle" drugs we had in our little bag was SubQ epinephrine. SubQ stands for subcutaneous administration of the drug. In other words, the needle would be stuck just under the skin and not in the muscle. The drug was injected into the arms of patients who had had anaphylactic reactions to...whatever. In many cases, it might be a bee sting or ingestion of a food like peanut butter or seafood.

The last one I will include in this category is adenosine, sometimes sold as Adenocard. It normally took about five to fifteen minutes to take effect. We would bolus six milligrams IV push quick and then flush with a bolus of saline. The anticipated result would be converting an abnormally rapid heart rate, such as paroxysmal supraventricular tachycardia. The heart would come to a complete standstill, reset the electrical system, and restart. I know this sounds rather radical to some, but by God it worked more often than not. Occasionally, we would have to do it twice. I remember the first time I gave it to a patient. I told him he was going to go to sleep for a short time and then he would feel better. When his heart stopped, I couldn't take my eyes off the EKG. I almost shit my pants; then his heart started back up. He felt better, and I didn't have to clean my pants.

INCIDENT FORTY-FIVE:
"WHAT GOES UP MUST COME DOWN"

It had been a busy day. I had worked on two cardiac arrest calls, a murder-suicide, and an opioid overdose. When I came in that night, the lieutenant asked what my count was for the day and my reply was, "A total of five. Two for the funeral home, and three for the medical examiner's office." Then he said, "Well it's livin'." Then he smiled and added, "for some."

Some days were harder than others and this one had been particularly brutal. One of the cardiac arrest calls was for an infant. I arrived to find the crew working a code blue. They were all sweating profusely due to the ambient temperature in the house. I spoke with the baby's mother to try to get some medical background or at least a history of this occurrence. I was advised that the baby did not have any medical history that was pertinent to this situation. The mother stated between tears," I only went to sleep for…for a few minutes." I asked her where the baby was when she was sleeping. Her reply was chilling. She exclaimed, "He was right beside me, on the sofa." She then continued, "I woke up and he wasn't moving. I mean he wasn't breathing!" It's very difficult to speak with a mother that has just lost her child. I continued, "Do you remember what time you went to sleep and what time you woke up?" She replied, "There is no way I was asleep more than an hour to an hour and a half." I thought to myself: plenty of time to accidentally suffocate the baby. The crew put the baby in the back of the medic unit and continued working the code blue to the ED. The ED called the code off within a few minutes after the crew's arrival. I waited with the mother and continued to speak with her—trying to console, but at the same time trying to get as much information as I could about the incident. She was sitting in a chair at the kitchen table, and I took a seat beside her. I told her the police would be arriving soon and that I was so sorry, but I needed to inform her that her baby had been pronounced dead at the hospital. She screamed, "The police?" I went on to inform her that it was normal for the police to become involved with any death, and I waited until the police officers arrived and turned the scene over to them.

The baby was later transported to the state morgue for autopsy. The findings of the medical examiner's chief pathologist was that the infant boy had died from suffocation due to co-sleeping.

I wish I could say I only saw a couple of accidental suffocations over the years, but that would be a lie. I have seen many, too many to count. Too many to forget.

With that and the rest of the day's calls sticking in my mind, I crawled into my bunk and flipped on the TV. About twenty minutes later, Audie, my battalion chief, lay down on his bunk bed across the room.

The layout of the room had to do with the number of shifts in the department. There were three southside battalion chiefs and three EMS captains citywide, thus six beds in the room. Only one of the chiefs and one captain stayed in the bedroom at a time. The rest of the crews from the ladder company, the engine company, and the medic unit slept in a huge general bedroom.

I have no idea how long Audie had been in the room, but suddenly there was a noise from the ceiling and almost at the same time it appeared that someone or something had moved every slat on the blinds on one of the windows. The window, by the way, was closed, so no wind was available at the time.

I sat bolt upright as did Audie. The only light in the room was the TV, so I popped up and turned on the overhead light. To our surprise, we found insulation all over the beds. At first it just did not make any sense, then I looked up at the ceiling and saw a hole with insulation sticking out of it.

Keep in mind this station had been in use for over a hundred years and tales of old departed firefighters always circulated. If I am going to be honest, the ghost thing—even though I don't believe in them—was on my mind at the time. So, I walked over to the window in question and carefully examined it. The window was intact, and the window blinds seemed OK too. My eyes then fell upon the windowsill to find the culprit.

A slug from a forty-five-caliber pistol lay quietly on the sill. I picked it up, looked at Audie, and said, "We've got incoming!"

The slug had crashed through the roof and then the ceiling. It then struck the metal frame at the top of the window. I later found a dent where it had contacted the window frame. The big ole piece of lead then fell straight down slightly bending every slat on the blinds."

Audie notified the police that we had taken incoming fire from a pistol and that so far only one round had been found.

An officer responded to the station, and we talked for a bit about what were the chances of us taking a round through the ceiling. I wanted to keep the slug, but the officer said no. He stated that he would keep it as evidence, and if they could find a ballistics match, they might find the person who pulled the trigger. He also said they had, just prior to the bullet hitting our bedroom, received a call for shots fired not far away. I asked where the shots fired call was located, and to my surprise, it was the same location of one of my daytime offices at another station.

Great, I thought, someone shooting from one station to the other, which was about eight and a half blocks. Again, what are the chances?

About a month later, that officer came knocking at our door with a bit of news. He stated that the guy who shot the forty-five-caliber round into our bedroom had been caught. Apparently, he had been involved in another misstep of justice, and they connected his pistol to our slug. He had confessed to shooting his pistol up in the air, just for fun.

I still did not get to keep the forty-five-caliber slug. I thought that would have made a great item to place on my desk at work for a conversation piece.

INCIDENT FORTY-SIX:
"NICE DOGGY...NOT"

This small group of stories all have the same theme: dogs that were not nice. Now make no mistake, I love dogs. Hell, I even love cats! But back to the topic of unfriendly dogs.

One could imagine a multitude of situations where dogs might become angry. Unfortunately, I don't have to imagine; I remember vividly.

The Throne

This first incident involves a call that came to us of a possible heart attack. The normal compliment of apparatuses was dispatched. That initially involved a medic unit with a paramedic and an EMT as well as an engine company with four personnel on board. At least one of the four would normally be a medic, along with the others, all EMS-trained up to be EMTs or better.

I heard the call go out and simply listened to the crews chime in. Engine-9 and Medic-9 responding to 574 Billings Street,NW. The dispatcher acknowledged and again I listened. I was not required for the initial response and probably would not be needed at all.

Within just a few minutes they both marked on scene. It took only about two minutes for the silence to be interrupted by the captain from Engine-9 calling for RS-1 to assist. I was already in my vehicle, out and about, so I flipped on my lights, hit the siren, and went. I advised dispatch that I was en route to the scene with an ETA of approximately five minutes. She then acknowledged my radio traffic.

The paramedic from Medic-9 keyed up his portable radio and called, asking me to step it up. Generally, I would respond pretty much the same to all calls, most of the time. But when an experienced medic asked me to hurry…well, I might have pressed a bit harder on the accelerator.

As I pulled up to the front of the house, I marked on scene, exited my vehicle, and walked toward the residence. The engine captain met me at the porch and advised me that they had a terrible circumstance.

He said, "This poor old guy is turning blue, and we can't get to him." My immediate response was something like, "Why the hell not?" He blurted out, "It's the damn dog. It will not let us get anywhere near the man."

I figured it must be a big ass mean dog to keep six strong, burly firefighters from accessing their patient. He told me it was safe to go in but not near the man. I walked into the house to find this poor old guy, naked as a jaybird, sitting on a Porta-Pot in the middle of his living room. He was barely conscious, and there was a little brown Chihuahua sitting under the pot. I started to walk towards the patient, and the dog squirted out with his teeth gleaming and a ferocious growl. I took a step back, and the dog retreated to his spot under the pot. The man's neighbor was the one who had alerted 9-1-1, and he told us that the dog was always very protective but that he had never seen him like this before.

Every time anyone got near, the dog attacked and then retreated again. I took off my turnout coat and tried to swipe the raging animal out of the way, and he grabbed my coat for a moment and then went back to the sanctity under the throne on which his master sat. The master who was still turning blue, I might add.

I started to just dropkick the dog, and then a thought came into my overly intelligent brain. I told one of the firefighters to open a nearby bedroom door and be ready to close it. I took a blanket from a bed, and as I shoved the blanket near the dog, he grabbed hold and I tried to wrap him up in the blanket but failed. This, however, did appear to be a viable possibility. I just needed to act a bit more expeditiously. I tossed the blanket at the foot of the Porta-Pot one more time, and the dog took a good bite and held on longer this time. I wrapped the savage little beast up in the blanket, and as I threw the blanket and dog through the bedroom door, the firefighter manning his post closed the door. We were free from that snarly little mongrel.

The personnel from Medic-9 and Engine-9 took care of the gentleman, and last I heard he survived his near-death experience as did the rest of us. OK, maybe ours was not a near-death experience, but it was damned close.

Regular Customer

The next incident took place at a nondescript house on the corner of a block that virtually every paramedic and FF/EMT came to know and seriously not love.

My first encounter was once again at the request of the personnel already on scene. A young lady had called 9-1-1, requesting an ambulance due to chest pain. The medic unit responded, and upon arrival they noted a screened-in porch. The dispatcher had told the crew the patient was alone and to come in, the door was open.

As soon as the screen door was pulled open and the first person started to walk onto the porch, a midsized, brown-and-tan, multibreed hound shot out of his doghouse on the porch. The dog was extremely serious about taking a bite out of something or someone. Fortunately, the chain around his neck was just shy of reaching the screen door, but no one could get by and there was no other way into the house. They still had a patient apparently in need of medical assistance, so they called for me to respond. Before I marked en route, I notified animal control to respond as well.

I arrived prior to animal control and had dispatch call back the subject who had initially called 9-1-1. I had the dispatcher ask permission to break a window if the caller was in dire straits. She declined and advised that her father would soon be there and to wait for him.

The father and animal control arrived simultaneously. The young lady's father contained the dog, and we went into the house as animal control cleared back into service.

The medical team from Medic-5 assessed the patient and concluded that she was not having cardiac-related pain but appeared to be having a panic attack instead.

During the early days of our system, the medic on scene was allowed to turn down a patient who they believed did not require emergency transport. Later, that responsibility fell on the shoulders of the Rescue Supervisor. The medic and I conferred and agreed the caller did not require transport. I spoke with the father, and he even agreed and said she had a long history of making inappropriate calls to 9-1-1 where they used to live. I then thanked him for his candor. Medic-5 and I cleared and went back into service.

A couple of days later, on my very next shift, a call came in on the radio, and I noticed it was from the same location. I called dispatch and asked if she could find out if the father was home, and I marked en route to that location.

Upon my arrival, I saw the crew standing outside once again due to an angry reception at the screen door. The father apparently had been to the grocery store and returned soon after I arrived. We once again had the gentleman restrain the snarling little critter, and in we went. If you have ever worked EMS, you probably know what happened next. You guessed it, she had the same complaint and the same symptoms. I had the medic and EMT check her over extremely well, and everything came back normal. I told the crew to clear, and I stayed to talk with the "patient" and her father. We sat down and talked about the importance of calling 9-1-1 when an emergency existed and the dangers of doing the opposite. We also talked about what constituted an emergency and what did not. I advised the father that I was going to instruct our dispatcher to advise anyone responding to their location to wait outside, regardless of the nature of the call, unless they could verify the dog had been put up or restrained in some manner. Thus, creating a safe environment for the first responders. He stated that he understood, as did his daughter.

Yep, you old dinosaurs of EMS could probably write the rest of this story. We received an untold number of calls from the daughter, many of which the father was unaware. When the father knew about the 9-1-1 request from his daughter, he took the dog off the porch and placed him in a pickup truck parked beside the house. If memory serves, our system probably transported the young lady five or six times out of the hundred or so requests. The times that she was transported, the ED would normally check her over and send her home. Hypochondria is in fact a real thing, but we could not afford to have a medic unit tied up on a BS call when another person with a real emergency might be in need. Our office sent numerous letters and threats of incarceration, to no avail.

The deputy chief and I even paid them a couple of visits and spoke with the father and the daughter. These conversations were indeed adversarial. We advised that the next time a request for an ambulance was made from this residence, the medic unit would respond as would the EMS supervisor and a police office. If she did not require emergency transport, she would be placed under arrest for false 9-1-1 calls. We had documented all the calls and all the dead-end conversations, not to mention the risk to our responders, running emergency, plus a violent dog ready to pounce as soon as the screen door opened.

Nothing seemed to work until one day the 9-1-1 calls stopped. I'm sure your imagination is running wild by now—OK, maybe not. Did she die; did he kill her? Did the dog turn on both and devour them? I guess I could go on with this BS for a few more lines, but I will not. They simply moved out of town—I'm sure to another unsuspecting location with a 9-1-1 system, ready to start all over.

Fire Pit

Do you remember seeing cool photos of a fire truck in a parade with a Dalmatian riding alongside the firefighter? I do too, but firefighters and dogs do not always necessarily make good bedfellows.

This time the request for equipment was for an apartment fire. A full complement of apparatuses responded: Engine-2, Ladder-2, Medic-2, Engine-5, Medic-5, Battalion Chief-2, and Rescue Supervisor-1 all responded. All the equipment from Station 2 arrived at the same time, and BC-2 marked up as Incident Command (IC). E-5, M-5, and I in RS-1 arrived about a couple of minutes after the others.

The fire was working on taking out a couple of apartments, and an interior attack was in progress. All the occupants of the two involved apartments were out, and everyone else from the building was accounted for.

I had been placed in charge of the medical division, and up to that point, no one was injured and the fire was almost under control. I had the personnel from M-5 pull out some basic equipment and place it on a stretcher just in case.

I was standing not far from the building, and the IC asked me to obtain a bit of information from the person who had been occupying the apartment of origin. I saw the man standing maybe fifty feet away, and I started to walk toward him. The next thing I knew, I had a white-and-tan pit bull slowly walking toward me. No tail wagging was noted, and the dog was literally staring me down. I stopped and the dog did not. The only things I had in my hands were a pen and a clipboard. Then I realized I was wearing a fire helmet, so I took off the helmet and prepared to go to war. The owner, who happened to be the gentleman I was about to talk to, yelled for me not to move. The following is exactly what I heard him say, "Don't fucking move, he WILL attack. He WILL jump you!" OK, I did not move an inch. The dog continued to walk toward me, and I called back to the owner and said, "I WILL knock the shit out of your dog, you better contain him!" I then keyed my radio mic and requested PD to my location for a possible dog attack.

About the time the officer got to me, the owner was able to grab the dog by its collar. The officer was ready, willing, and able to take out the dog. The owner was instructed to place the dog in a secure location and then return for Q-and-A.

I would like to reiterate, I love dogs, I love cats, I love just about all animals. But—you knew a but was coming, didn't you—I could have been bitten, and the dog was going to suffer a blow to the head with that helmet with all that I had to offer. Thank God, it did not come to that.

INCIDENT FORTY-SEVEN:
"I'M NOT TALKING TO YOU"

"Engine-10, Medic-10, Engine-5, RS-1 respond to a vehicle accident at the off-ramp on I-881 to Burger Road," the dispatcher said, before continuing, "Bystander advised, vehicle overturned, time 14:28."

The captain riding the seat marked up with, "Engine-10, Medic-10 en route to off-ramp from I-881 to Burger Road." Dispatch acknowledged and gave the time. Then the captain on E-5 stated, "Engine-5 en route to off-ramp from I-881 to Burger Road." Once again, the dispatcher stated the time. It was then my turn. Generally speaking, the officer who was ultimately in charge of the call chimed in last. I simply stated, "RS-1 en route auto accident on Burger Road, off-ramp from I-881." She again acknowledged and gave the time and advised PD was en route.

I realize there is a great deal of redundancy in the radio traffic, but keep in mind, the apparatuses responding, as well as their respective times, are critical to document. A delayed response for instance would be heavily critiqued in an after-action report. The company would have to have one hell of a good excuse if they either had a delayed response or even worse, no response at all. Keep in mind, just because it's a 9-1-1 service does not make it foolproof. Mistakes happen. Unfortunately, mistakes during a 9-1-1 response could cost someone's life.

The captain on Engine-10, upon arrival, marked Engine-10 and Medic-10 on the scene. He also advised the location and the fact that the vehicle was overturned. The captain on Engine-10 then assumed IC. Engine-5 was our primary extrication apparatus. Prior to Engine-5 arriving, the IC gave the engine company pertinent information over the air, so when they arrived, the captain on Engine-5 would know where to position his apparatus and basically what equipment they might need for the patient extrication.

Engine-5 arrived and once again dispatch acknowledged with the time. I had to travel a bit further, so I brought up the rear, so to speak, and arrived a couple of minutes later. I walked up to the accident scene to see a Chevy sedan on its side. Engine-10 had already pulled a line and was in the process of charging the hose with water. Medic-10 had already made contact with the young lady in the upended vehicle. The prospective patient was still belted in on the driver's side, and there was no one else in the car.

The vehicle was damaged but not as bad as one would expect with it being on its side. The interior of the vehicle was intact, and the airbags had deployed.

I noticed as I approached the subject's car another vehicle had pulled up to the scene and parked on the side of the off-ramp.

An elderly lady exited the car and started walking toward the active scene. I took my eyes off the approaching female and asked the lead medic what the situation was. He advised that the young lady did not appear to be in any difficulty other than being kind of stuck in the seat belt. Engine-5's personnel stabilized the vehicle to insure it would not move to either side. The IC approached me and said the young lady in the car was refusing medical assistance due to no injuries. As the car was now stable, one of the firefighter/EMTs crawled inside the car and was holding manual cervical stabilization and communicating how they were going to get her out. She told him that she wasn't hurt but was just stuck and if he would get her out of the seat belt, she would be fine.

An additional assessment was then about to take place as the medic also accessed the vehicle. They gradually lowered her from the seat belt and carefully checked her out. The twenty-three-year old's vitals were all good, and she had no complaints. The word was from the medic, no apparent injuries and she was refusing medic assistance.

Looking at the car and the position it ended up in, it appeared to have been a slow roll up to its side, and we all felt comfortable with her signing a refusal and allowing her to deal with the police officer on scene.

Remember that lady who had parked on the side of the ramp? Well, here we go. As the medic was explaining the refusal and that he would need her to sign, the elderly lady walked directly to the medic and the young lady from the car and told her she was going to the hospital. The young lady turned and said, "Granny, I don't need to go, I'm fine." Now we understood the connection between the two. The sweet little old lady then said, "Bullshit, you are going, and they are taking you to the emergency room!" I walked over to the trio and said, "Excuse me ma'am, how can I help you?" Trying to distract her away from the medic and the young lady. She quickly turned and rather harshly said, "You can take her to the damn hospital!" I calmly responded with what I intended as educational information and stated, "Ma'am, she doesn't wish to go to the hospital, and we have found no reason for an emergency transport, plus she is about to sign a refusal." She walked over to the medic and grabbed the clipboard.

My patience was starting to run just a tad thin, and I said, "Ma'am, return the clipboard to the young man helping your granddaughter." She turned toward me, and I simply retrieved the clipboard and started speaking to the young lady, asking her if she understood everything that had been explained and if so, to go ahead and sign the refusal.

Well, let me tell you, granny did not appreciate that a bit, and she grabbed my jacket and yelled continually, claiming that we were going to take her granddaughter to the hospital. I told her not to grab me and to stand back while we were completing this discussion. I turned toward the young lady, and granny grabbed me again and I succinctly stated, "Ma'am, if you touch me again, I'll have that officer restrain you." The officer was watching the entire

272

fiasco, and he nodded to affirm he would remove granny if necessary. I once again turned to speak to the granddaughter, and you know what happened, right? Yep, granny did it again only this time she tried to pull me back, and I looked at the officer, and said, "She's all yours." Granny's eyes got about as big as saucers when the officer turned her around and gave her a nice shiny pair of bracelets. He then accompanied her, as she yelled, kicked at the officer, and cursed both of us, to the back seat of his patrol car.

Within moments, another patrol car showed up and granny was transferred and driven off to jail. I honestly did not anticipate they would take her off, but hey, I was not talking to her.

The pleasant young lady then signed the refusal, and we left the scene. I received a call from the second officer, and she asked me if I was interested in pressing any charges. I asked if they were charging her with anything, and the reply was "not unless you wish." I told her I was OK with not charging her, and I hoped she learned her lesson. I seriously doubt that she did.

INCIDENT FORTY-EIGHT:
"SPEED BUMP"

"Medic-10, Engine-10, RS-1—respond to the Raleigh Court Mall for a pedestrian struck by a vehicle. This will be in front of Luxor Book Store. 10:35."

The captain on Engine-10 shortly thereafter chimed in with "Engine-10, Medic-10 responding to Raleigh Court Mall at Luxor Book Store." The dispatcher acknowledged with the time: "10:37."

I quickly marked en route and asked if she had any further information, and she did not.

Due to the fact this call was in a mall parking lot, I responded but, quite frankly, anticipated being disregarded by the first arriving apparatus. Generally, the injuries to a pedestrian struck in a parking lot would turn out to be minor and would not require my presence on the scene.

Once again, I was on the other side of the city and my response time was going to be approximately ten to fifteen minutes, depending on traffic. Station 10, however, was not far from the mall.

As I continued driving, I heard the captain on Engine-10 mark both units on scene. I anticipated soon receiving confirmation that they could handle the call and that I could disregard

As I was about to pull off the interstate spur onto the road leading to the mall, I heard, "RS-1, Engine-10." I replied, "Engine-10, go ahead." They said, "RS-1, we are going to need you to continue and step it up." That was unexpected. Again, my intuition was way off.

I arrived about two minutes later. I climbed out of RS-1 to find all four men from Engine-10 and one of the paramedics from Medic-10 standing and looking at a lady on the pavement. The other medic was kneeling at the patient's head, holding cervical stabilization. They had already applied a cervical collar and had a non-rebreather O2 mask in place. You may remember Paramedic Williams from a previous chapter. She looked at the patient and then back at me. She said, "We are stuck. Every time we get near her, she screams, and I don't know how to fix this." I looked back at the patient again and then to Williams. I said, "We don't really have much of a choice. We must get her on the stretcher one way or the other."

Here is a trick I have used several times, and it does work, and it helps the patient. But it is not easy on the patient or the medic. I asked for one of the firefighter/EMTs to retrieve a pair of MAST trousers, and I loosely closed the Velcro closures. I put both of my arms into the bottom of the leg openings and pulled the trousers up high on my arms. I then twisted my arms as much as I could—and now the fun begins. I looked at the perplexed patient and said, "Ma'am, this is going to hurt like a son of a bitch for a few seconds, but I promise it will help you and make you feel better for your ride to the hospital."

Let me back up just a bit, no pun intended. When I arrived on this scene, I saw a police officer speaking with an elderly lady along with a couple of bystanders. I tapped the bystander on the shoulder and asked if he knew what had occurred.

Here's the story: one little, old, grey-haired lady hit another little, old, grey-haired lady who was in the crosswalk. That is bad enough, but it goes on. Several bystanders saw the woman fall after she was hit, and the car ran directly over her. A couple of the guys who were watching in horror beat on the car's window and yelled at the driver to stop, but she continued as the victim was forcefully rolled underneath the vehicle. She rolled and twisted, and her legs were broken, and her pelvis was crushed. They finally got the driver to stop but not until the human pretzel was spit out from the rear of the vehicle.

The problem the patient presented to the first responders was that her legs were so twisted she looked more like a rag doll instead of the little old lady she was.

Now to continue: I picked up her legs by the feet, and as I pulled traction on her legs, I untwisted them. She let out with a blood-curdling scream from hell. After I had her legs straight and with manual traction on both, I had a FF/EMT inflate the trousers, which would keep her legs and the pelvis as stable as possible.

We rolled her and placed her on a back board, then placed the backboard to the stretcher. As Medic-10's personnel picked her up to roll her into the back of the ambulance, she looked at me in a way I don't think I can quite describe. She then said, "You were right, it does feel a lot better."

Paramedic Williams transported the patient to the nearest Level one trauma center and advised the hospital that this would be a Gold Alert. After the reasonably short trip, Medic-10 showed up at the Emergency Department, and Paramedic Williams had started two large-bore IV lines, monitored the cardiac status of the patient, and as she always did, comforted her patient.

INCIDENT FORTY-NINE:
"DEAD ON ARRIVAL"

If I may, let me recap a few things to help keep everything in perspective. My career with EMS, fire, and the medical examiner's office covered thirty-five years. I was a volunteer for about eight years, and a couple of those overlapped with my first paid EMS job with an ambulance transport company. I worked that first EMS job as a cardiac technician while attending school to obtain my National Registry of Emergency Medical Technicians-Paramedic certification.

Once the NREMT-P certification was obtained, I became gainfully employed with the city system I have mentioned before. That career lasted twenty-five years, and during a portion of that, I worked as a paramedic preceptor for a local health science college. I also flew with the trauma center's air ambulance program.

After my retirement from the city's fire-EMS department, I worked as an investigator with the ME's office. That stint of employment lasted four years and added exponentially to my experience with the deceased.

I find it difficult to recall a lot of the DOAs. There were simply so many that they eventually kind of ran together and became blurred. A few stood out for one reason or another, and several I have chronicled previously in this book.

The sheer numbers of human beings I have pronounced dead from gunshot wounds is staggering: parents shot by their children, generally due to either child or spousal abuse; or children shot accidentally, simply because the gun owner was not responsible enough to keep the weapon in a safe place away from small kids. One of my pet peeves was that the legal system very often would not charge the parent in these circumstances, or the sentence would be so light no one else took notice. Therefore, it did not act as a deterrent.

Shootings involving two or more young adults were common. Pistols by far were the most customary weapons of choice. They were easy to come by if the purchaser didn't care from whom or where the weapon came.

That reminds me of cities that have said that firearm buyback programs would reduce crime. I'm sure all the criminals out there turned in their pistols and rifles for a couple of hundred dollars of groceries. What do the officials not understand about the word "criminal?" Criminals generally don't obey the law. They generally don't go to a gun store to purchase a brand spanking new six-hundred-dollar pistol. They don't buy guns where they are subjected to a background check. All these proclamations made by government officials to decrease crime by increasing restraints on law-abiding citizens are futile, in my opinion. Let me climb off my bandwagon and get back to the topic of dead folks.

Guns, I hope you realize, are not the only way people kill each other or themselves, for that matter. Just about any object can be used as a weapon. A hammer, an ashtray, a bottle, a rock, a knife, a frying pan, a car, a rope, a metal pipe. I could go on and on, but I believe you probably get the picture. People have been done in by just about every object on earth. Not to mention a chicken bone, a plastic bag, a fish bone, or even a piece of meat. The possibilities, including natural causes, are virtually infinite.

A DOA is an easy call for a paramedic. It usually involves much less paperwork than a dynamic call where the patient is actively worked on the scene and transported to the hospital. The police probably end up with less paperwork as well. Countless times we would interact with the police. Sometimes the officer would arrive first, and sometimes it would be one of us, depending on how the call originally came in.

I guarantee all of us have been exposed to death of one sort or another from an early age. As a child, it may have been the loss of a family pet or a grandparent or sometimes even a parent or sibling. First responders are not exposed to large quantities of death in a short amount of time like military members in a warzone. Instead, our burden accumulates over many years. When I retired from my stint as a death investigator, I was amazed when I realized that a week had gone by, and then a month, and eventually a year, and I had not dealt with death.

A fresh DOA was always welcomed over a body that had been unnoticed for a few days or weeks. The human body decays just like a dead animal on the side of the road. The odor is very similar, and some of us got used to it and some did not.

Drowning victims were a bit unique when they had been underwater for an extended time. The old term "bloat and float" was used quite frequently among first responders. When a body is underwater for a while, the gases that form in the body create a buoyancy and will often bring the body to the surface.

I'm going to hit on the five basic stages of decomposition:

Fresh is the first stage, during which there is a loss of color in the skin, or pallor mortis. In my experience, light-skinned people become rather pale and dark-skinned people become somewhat ashen in color. Rigor mortis and livor mortis are also within the "fresh" category. Rigor refers to the body becoming stiff, and livor has to do with the pooling of blood in dependent parts of the body due to gravity.

Bloat is the next stage, during which proteins in the body decompose, which leads to a breakdown of the body's cells and tissues, the liquefaction of the organs, and the creation and buildup of gasses that give this stage its name—and a rather foul odor.

Active decay is when insects come into the picture. Different types of insect activity can assist investigators in determining the length of time since death. For instance, blow flies are one of the first insects to arrive at a corpse, and the development stages of their maggots on a body can be used as a timeline as well.

Advanced decay creates major changes in the appearance of the body. Most of the body will be discolored, and the decomposition of the body is nearly complete.

Dry or skeletonized remains appear dramatically discolored. The bloat is complete, the tissues of the body have collapsed on themselves, and the skeleton is very pronounced. Quite often, the skin will be leathery in appearance.

I recall one time, with EMS, we encountered a body that had been inside a very hot house for about a week or so. When I arrived, I saw one officer with a cigar hanging out of his mouth. I knew what that meant. He approached me outside and said that the body was bad off and that they had called the ME's office. He said he needed me to pronounce the subject dead. I opened the door, took a whiff, and said, "Yep, it's dead." The officer was not amused.

I went inside and looked at the bloated body and advised the officer that it was beyond my ability to revive the subject. Again, not amused. We looked around the house to see if we could find any medication bottles to give us a clue as to what might have happened to the gentleman. We found some paperwork with his presumed name and some medications. I obtained what information I could and went back into service. The officer would have to wait for the ME's investigator.

When possible, we would have some fun at the expense of a rookie police officer. Even the older officers would join in on the fun. If we had a body that needed to be turned over, and we knew the aroma would be strong, we would tell the rookie to stand over the body and turn it. I've seen more than one lose their cookies.

I remember this one sad guy on a park bench. It had been down in the teens that night, and first thing in the morning we were called for a possible DOA in a city park. Poor guy was frozen solid. No telling how long he had been there. Another frozen guy was found one time under a snow drift. Again, frozen like a big piece of ice.

In the ME's office we would have to leave them on a table and not in the cooler to let then thaw before the pathologist could perform an autopsy.

Unfortunately, I could go on and on. Once again, things that one cannot unsee.

INCIDENT FIFTY:
"BIRTHDAY PRESENT"

This incident is about one of the closest and best friends I have ever had. Neither Sarah nor her family, which included husband Bill, daughter Sharon, and son-in-law George, knew at the time how much they meant to me. Bill was a strong-minded, stubborn man with a heart of gold. He cared about his family, his rescue squad, and his faith. He proudly wore his badge, and even though his medical knowledge was not up to some standards, he was willing to pitch in and help in any way that was requested of him. George and Sharon took an enormous amount of time out of their busy schedules to volunteer. Sarah was one of the most intuitive individuals I have ever known. She would take her medical training and combine it with her kindness and love of life to help guide and nurture those around her. She had such a smile and a laugh that brightened up any dreary day. Did I mention that she was as, if not more, stubborn than Bill?

One day I came into work, and Sarah walked over to me, gave me a big hug, and said "Happy birthday." I didn't even know she knew it was my birthday. She handed me a Wisconsin laryngoscope set. It consisted of a handle and three blades. That was amazing, and it became one of the most-used pieces of medical equipment I carried over my entire medical career.

As a fledgling paramedic, I ran with many partners. Some were volunteers and others career based as I was. I rarely had to ask Sarah for anything. She would know the next step and virtually always was ahead of the game. The close relationship one builds with one's partner working through death and dying scenarios daily is extremely strong. I say this to impress on you, the reader, how much this lady meant to me. This older, heavyset, black lady and I had nothing in common, but at the same time, we had everything in common. I don't remember how many years she had on me, but it was not just a few.

As time went on, the city paramedic program grew, and the volunteer system began to wane. After approximately ten years, the EMS and fire department in the city merged into one program. The volunteers hung on in one station as the career side pretty much took over. It was a natural progression. The demands for continued medical education were just too high for most of the volunteers to keep up with and maintain a career of their own. With that said, Bill, Sarah, Sharon, and George hung up their uniforms when their volunteer crew disbanded. Over the years, I kept up with Sarah and Bill. I knew where they lived, and occasionally, I would drop by, sit on their porch, and have a cup of coffee and reminisce.

One day, I was driving around town, hopping from station to station, doing my regular rounds, when the tones went off and the dispatcher advised of a person not breathing and without a pulse. The address that was given was familiar. It took a moment to sink in, but I suddenly realized it was Sarah and Bill's home. I turned on my red flashing strobe lights and hit the siren. I'm not sure how fast I was driving, but it was damn fast. I arrived just before the ambulance and engine company. To my horror, it was Sarah!

I immediately keyed my mic and advised "Code Blue, Code Blue." My training clicked in and somehow, I was for the moment, able to function and deal with what was unfolding right before my eyes. George was there, and if memory serves, he was doing CPR when I arrived. The ambulance and engine company arrived soon thereafter, and we applied every bit of knowledge we had acquired over the years, but she just would not respond. She had developed diabetes and heart disease over the years, and no matter how hard we tried, she was lost.

All I could say to her family was that I was so sorry we couldn't help. Of all the people on Earth not to be able to help, why her? I openly sobbed. As I write these words, I feel the profound sadness I felt that day and for years to follow.

Bill was out of town on that day. I didn't have the heart to go to the funeral, and I didn't have the guts to talk to Bill for almost two years. Finally, I drove back up to the house where Bill then lived alone and knocked on the door. I was welcomed with open arms. Bill gave me a big hug and said how good it was to see me. All I could muster was that I was so damn sorry I couldn't help Sarah that day, and I cried once again. He said, "You did everything you could. It just wasn't to be." We sat on the porch for about an hour talking about the "Good ole Days." I apologized for not coming to her funeral and for staying away for so long. I told him I just couldn't face him knowing I was unable to get her back. I told him I had used the birthday present he and Sarah had given me many years before on Sarah that day when I intubated her. We made small talk for a bit longer and I drove off.

I spoke with Bill not long ago when I was writing this book. I asked if it would be OK if I used his families first names in my book and I told him about the stories in which they were included. He said he would be proud and that he knew Sarah would have been too.

EPILOGUE

Humor is sometimes funny only to the person attempting to be funny. It can also catch on if all involved are on the same page, so to speak.

For example, imagine a group of first responders, predominantly paramedics and EMTs, digging through a collapsed building and searching for the remains of several people. I assure you they will be extremely solemn while cameras or other people not in the business are around. When they are all by themselves—well, they are not so dignified.

I remember digging around just like that, and when someone would find a foot or another body part, an inappropriate comment would emerge. Funny, yes? Maybe not, but when ordinary people are doing extraordinary things, they use humor as a major defense mechanism. We always realized we could not say things like that around victims' family members on the scene, but we often let loose when we were among our own kind.

We made off-color remarks on a regular basis. Remember when the lieutenant in my station would ask me how many I had killed that day? He meant no disrespect to me or to the dead. It was simply an attempt to keep things as light as possible.

Mental health for the EMS community is kind of hit-and-miss. There are some departments that have dedicated programs, but there is also a lot of hesitancy to take part. I've personally lost a couple of fellow paramedics due to suicide. One I still have a hard time dealing with. He had the opportunity to talk to anyone he wished, but he just chose not to talk. Instead, he put a shotgun in his mouth and left behind a great little family.

One thing EMS left me with, after thirty-five years of carrying people up and down stairs and lifting them into the back of an ambulance or into a helicopter, is the toll it's taken on my body. I have had six back surgeries, two cervical surgeries, and a total hip replacement. I am the proud owner of thirty-four screws, six rods—two of which are twenty inches long—and six cages, all in my spine.

Back to humor: I have found that humor allowed me to let things out that I couldn't afford to keep in. Remember how I keep saying one cannot unsee some things? Well, really one cannot unsee any of it; it stays with you, and if you let it, it will haunt you. Talking to a co-worker is a good thing, but even better is talking to a person trained in how to help the pain let go its mighty grip. I have been told that first responders are now being treated for post-traumatic stress disorder, or PTSD. When I was in the department, that wasn't even a thought.

I would like to end this group of stories on a positive note. B flat—that was always one of my favorites. Thank you for reading my thoughts, and may God bless.

#8 P. 46-5   P 35 4 LEVELS OF TRIAGE

P. 73 DIFF. B/T EMT + PARAMEDIC. + EMS
         WHAT IS ORDER OF TRAINING?
                                    MEDIC
P. 164 RATS
#28 KNIFE IN NOSE!
P. 183 EMS FIGHT FIRES?

P 292

Made in the USA
Columbia, SC
22 February 2023